AGAVE SUNSETS
Treasured Tales of Baja

A compilation of 50 stories and tips for traveling in Baja

by Ann Hazard
Author of COOKING WITH BAJA MAGIC
and CARTWHEELS IN THE SAND

Renegade Enterprises
Solana Beach, CA
November 2002

Library of Congress Cataloguing in Publication Data

Hazard, Ann
Agave Sunsets

A Renegade Enterprises Book
I. Title: Agave Sunsets
        ISBN 0-9653223-3-5
1. Travel & Travel Guides

Front Cover Photo by Ann Hazard
Story Photos by:Terry Hauswirth and Ann Hazard
unless otherwise noted
Edited by Sue and Jim Graham
Book and Cover Design by Colleen Taylor
Back cover author photo by Kim Boeck

See last page for ordering information

Other books by Ann Hazard:

Cooking With Baja Magic—Mouth-Watering Meals from the Kitchens and Campfires of Baja
Cartwheels in the Sand—Baja California, Four Women and a Motor Home

Dedication

This book is dedicated to the people of Mexico,
both native and expatriate
whose generosity of spirit, humor and corazón
inspire me continuously.

"Ann Hazard's new book, *Agave Sunsets*, is a must-read for Baja Aficionados, or anyone even mildly curious about Mexico. It's fun, informative and I promise that you'll fall in love with the people and places she describes."

—Laura Wong, *Baja Tourist Guide*

"Grab yourself a cold cerveza, kick back and treat yourself to a happy hour ... or three. Reading *Agave Sunsets* is like visiting with an old Baja buddy ... reliving great trips and laughing as you compare notes on your adventures."

—Jennifer Redmond, *Sea of Cortez Review*

"When Ann Hazard whisks you away to Baja, you have no choice but to come along for the ride. Her love of Mexico is so contagious it leaves you feeling as though you're with her, exploring that piece of paradise she calls home."

—Jean Gillette, *Coast News*

"In *Agave Sunsets* Ann Hazard's profound love for Baja becomes contagious. Her artfully spun tales—part personal vignette, part travel guide—will draw you into that enchanting experience that is purely Baja. From the Hat Party at Gordos in La Bufadora to tasting premier tequilas at Pancho's in Cabo San Lucas, the stories will make you nostalgic for old friends and haunts and yearn for those ever-new Baja adventures. Don't wait! Start reading now! It's definitely the 'Baja fix' you've been needing."

—Carol Kramer, *Discover Baja Travel Club*

Acknowledgments

My sincerest thanks and appreciation go to everyone whose stories make up this book—my family, Terry Hauswirth, my friends and neighbors in La Bufadora, Baja California, my many wonderful Mexican amigos on both sides of the border ... and all the folks I've met along the way in my travels and adventures.

Special thanks go to Jim Kydd, publisher of the *Coast News*, and my editor, Michelle Kaskovich. Many of these stories were first published in your paper. To Laura Wong, editor of the *Baja Tourist Guide,* Mayté Rodriguez, publisher of *Baja Traveler Magazine*, Liz Fautsch, editor of *Cedros Review Magazine*, Charlie Arneson, general manager of Fox Studios Baja and Foxploration and Mike Crowell, my editor at the *San Diego Union-Tribune*. Mil gracias a ustedes también, amigos. Thank you for believing in me and publishing my work. Without you, this book would never have been born.

Last, but never least, I want to thank Sue and Jim Graham, the editors of *Agave Sunsets*. Your knowledge and patience has been a blessing and a gift.

Agave Sunsets
Table of Contents

Part One: In the Beginning ... Stories from Before

Part Two: Tales from La Bufadora

Places:

Adventures:

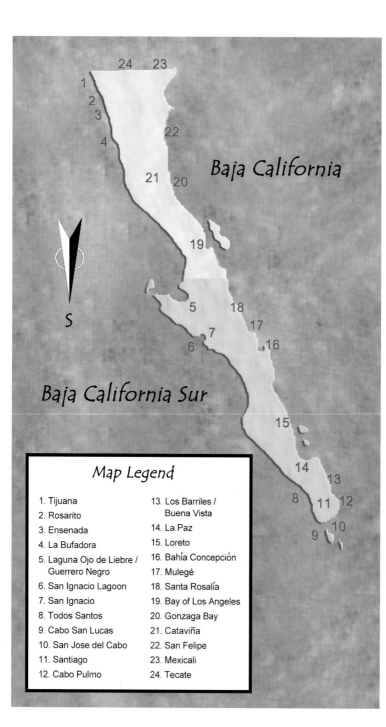

Baja California

Baja California Sur

S

24 23
1
2
3
22
4
21 20
19
5 18
17
7 16
6
15
14 13
8 11 12
9 10

Map Legend

1. Tijuana
2. Rosarito
3. Ensenada
4. La Bufadora
5. Laguna Ojo de Liebre / Guerrero Negro
6. San Ignacio Lagoon
7. San Ignacio
8. Todos Santos
9. Cabo San Lucas
10. San Jose del Cabo
11. Santiago
12. Cabo Pulmo
13. Los Barriles / Buena Vista
14. La Paz
15. Loreto
16. Bahía Concepción
17. Mulegé
18. Santa Rosalía
19. Bay of Los Angeles
20. Gonzaga Bay
21. Cataviña
22. San Felipe
23. Mexicali
24. Tecate

Togo and Pappy Hazard—Punta Banda 1934

Introduction

This is my third book about Baja California. I'm a third generation Baja Aficionada, as we Baja lovers are affectionately called. I've followed my grandfather's and parents' footsteps up and down this peninsula—the longest in the world—my whole life.

To me, Baja is a place of exquisite, pristine beauty set against a backdrop of near desolation. It's a place of endless cactus-inhabited hills, sunny skies and see-through aquamarine waters that teem with brightly colored fish. It's a place where hot springs bubble up to the ocean floor, burning my toes when I dance in the waves under the light of the moon. It's a place where gray whales come each year to give birth to their young; a place of boisterous, yet achingly beautiful Mariachi music. It's a smiling place of real-life cowboys and surprise oases, a place where people help each other—partly due to a necessity born out of isolation, but even more so because they care about and take joy in one another.

I am passionate about all things Mexican, and I've always felt more at home in this country than in my own. I've had a house in La Bufadora (actually, I've owned either all or part of three different places at three different times) since 1994. I practically raised my kids there. I plan to make it my home base as soon as Derek's off to college in a few years.

If you aren't a Mexico fanatic, you may not know what an agave is. There are two on the cover of this book. I took that photo in January 2002 from the edge of my patio in La Bufadora. Agaves are common all over Mexico. In La Bufadora, they dot the hillsides. Near Guadalajara they're grown to make tequila. They're squat plants that look like the top of a pineapple, with dusky green leaves. When they're about five or six years old, they sprout a single shaft that can reach up to six feet high. From its top bursts a flower with a multitude of bright yellow blossoms. After a few months, the flowers dry up and turn gray, but they stand tall, even in death, for years to come. The two on the cover bloomed the year before I took the photo.

The most famous species of agave is the blue agave or Agave Tequilana Weber, from which tequila is made. To me, the agave symbolizes Mexico. It's not in a hurry. It's dramatic when flowering, life sustaining (many *piñas*—cores—are edible, not just fermentable), prolific, it's the source of tequila ... and ... it looks dynamite at sunset.

Agave Sunsets is a metaphor that captures the essence of Mexico—my adopted country.

Nina and John Wayne, La Paz Airport 1961

Getting to the Root of It All
1890 (or Thereabouts)

My grandpa, "Pappy" Hazard, came to San Diego from
Arizona in the 1890s. A real-life cowboy, he raised cattle on ranches
spanning both sides of the border. This was back when there was no
real border, when immigration wasn't legal or illegal and the only
thing that divided our two countries was a lonely outpost on a dirt road
going—as Jimmy Buffett would say—"South." Pappy made his living
building highways, and in his spare time he hung out with people like
Erle Stanley Gardner. In case you haven't heard of Erle, he created
Perry Mason. He was also hooked on Baja and explored the peninsula
by truck, homemade ATV, helicopter, airplane and even a blimp. He
wrote several entertaining books about his escapades that you can find
in public libraries. Pappy's in one of them—*Mexico's Magic Square.*
In that book, published in 1968, these old dudes in their 80s explored

the remote areas between Tijuana, Ensenada, Tecate, San Felipe and Mexicali. They camped. They rode horses. They cruised off-road on homemade ATVs called "Butterflies" and "Grasshoppers." Pappy, a notoriously lucky poker player, whipped them all at cards, and Erle documented it.

My dad, "Togo," was born in 1922. His first trip to Baja was in 1931. This was back when it took all day to get from Tijuana to Ensenada on a windy little dirt road. The only access to Punta Banda, where Pappy had a fishing shack, was via a road that could only be negotiated at low tide. Otherwise it was under water. A far cry from the easy two-hour drive these days....

My mom, Dorothy, swore she'd never had her toes off Wilshire Boulevard until she graduated from high school. She wasn't very out-doorsy, but that didn't stop my dad from taking her to Baja in 1949, right after they got married. He was so excited, she told me. After all, he was taking her to one of his favorite fishing haunts and showing her his little Baja "casita" in Punta Banda. Just imagine her shock when he drove her down a long, winding dirt road and pulled up in front of a tiny, one room, dilapidated fishing shack with an outhouse in back! There were dust bunnies, daddy longlegs and spider webs everywhere. Everything—especially the sleeping bags—stunk, like very old, very dead fish. And stale sweat. They were full of sand too.

Obviously, my dad learned something that trip about places that are and are not "chick friendly." He was astute enough not to take her back to that shack. But he took her plenty of other places, and she grew to share his love of Mexico, and Baja in particular.

And me ... my first trip south was in 1957, when I was five. My first really big trip, though, was Easter Vacation, 1961, when I was eight and my sister, Nina, had just turned seven. We drove with our parents to the Tijuana airport and boarded a DC-6 bound for La Paz. Two-plus hours later we landed in a tiny airport pretty much out in the middle of nowhere. It was hot and dusty, and the air was ripe with unfamiliar, pungent smells. As we got off the plane, my dad grabbed both Nina's and my hands and pulled us over to this really tall gringo in a cowboy hat who was surrounded by people. He and my dad chat-ted a moment, then he crouched down and reached for both of us, just as my father whipped out his camera. Nina jumped onto his knee; I held back and stayed next to my dad.

It was John Wayne. Nina had her picture taken with him. Our whole week was as magical as that moment. We stayed at a hotel right on the bay. Every morning we went out sport fishing and anchored off a different beach on Isla Espiritú Santo for lunch. The first day out, Nina and I ate the entire picnic the hotel had packed for our family and the boat's crew—by 10:00. We weren't very popular that day. In fact, we had to cut the trip short because everyone (except the two of us) was ravenous.

Our mom taught us to snorkel on that trip. We swam through schools of yellow and gray-striped sergeant majors, spiny brown-spotted blowfish and rainbow-colored parrotfish. Nina, already showing signs of the scuba diver she'd become, dove at least twelve feet down to the reef below, searching the cracks between rocks for those elusive, darting flashes of fluorescent blue, yellow and turquoise—those tiny, exotic tropical fish that were the most spectacular of all. She found them, and an eel too. It leered at her from between two rocks, scaring Mom and me back to the boat.

We hunted for shells and picnicked on the sand. Nina and I ate tacos for breakfast every morning (we still do whenever possible) and every single piece of clothing we tossed onto the floor of our hotel room was washed, ironed and folded when we returned after our daily adventures. I met a girl named Frances Cuvi from Mexico City on this trip, and over the years we visited each other several times, staying in each other's homes, going to each other's schools and exploring each other's lives. We lost touch with each other after high school, but reconnected via the Internet a couple of years ago.

And my kids? I have two—Gayle and Derek. They're teenagers now, but both of them first traveled south of the border when they were in my belly. A couple of Christmases ago, Terry (the man in my life—I met him in Baja, of course) and I took them down and up Baja in a motor home. They've spent most of their vacations and lots of weekends since 1994 in La Bufadora. So ... that makes us four generations of Baja Aficionados.... And I can't forget the pets. We have two Mexican dogs right now. We had the coolest Baja cat imaginable too, but he had a fatal coyote encounter in the States.

Are you wondering why we're all so enamored with a foreign country? Well, let me share a couple of secrets about Mexicans. (These won't be secrets much longer—thanks to Presidente Vicente Fox and his *corazón*—incredible heart—for his country.) They believe that life is to be enjoyed, that integrity is paramount and that God and family are more important than money. They may live in a third world country, but guess what? They don't think they're deprived. They think we're fairly ridiculous with our obsession to hoard and discard possessions. Raise the hood of any ancient (but roadworthy) Baja *troque*— truck—and you will instantly appreciate Mexican ingenuity. These folks are more resourceful than you could ever imagine. They've raised recycling to an art form. And—they will use even the lamest of excuses to throw a fiesta. There are more holidays in Mexico than anywhere on earth, thanks to the ample number of saints's days and political events they have to celebrate. From gray-haired grannies to Pampers-clad toddlers, everyone gets into the spirit of revelry. Food abounds, cerveza and tequila flow and music blares.

* * * *

As a kid and as a teenager I loved going on trips to Mexico. It was my favorite kind of vacation. We got a camper as soon as they hit the market. We went camping on deserted beaches in northern Baja— places like Kilometer 181—and learned to make tortillas from a little lady who cooked over a stove made from a steel drum. We camped in the San Pedro Martir Mountains at the Meling Ranch and rode with the cowboys. We camped on the beach in San Felipe at the northern end of the Gulf of California. We flew into remote places like Bahía de Los Angeles and Mulegé—places that were unreachable except by air or dirt road until the Transpeninsular Highway (a.k.a. Mex 1) was paved in late 1973.

I still go south every chance I get. As of this writing my family has a nearly completed second home in La Bufadora, a few miles south of Ensenada, at the tail end of what has been labeled, "Baja's Romantic Gold Coast." We have electricity now, and a cell phone, but for six years we lived without phones, mail, computers and even television down there. Our water is hauled in by truck and stored in pilas, which are storage tanks—in our case, a concrete water tank. (No, we don't drink pila water, but I do brush my teeth in it. My theory on this is that a twice-daily dose of iffy water keeps my bacteria level Mexico-compatible.) If we want to visit neighbors, we spy on them first with our binoculars. Yes, you could definitely say we are a community of voyeurs. But it works. If we get a positive sighting, we strap on our hiking sandals and cruise on over for a visit.

It is against the backdrop of its mountains, deserts and endless beaches that we Baja Aficionados reconnect with the essence of who we are. I—like everyone else whose soul has been captured and forever held prisoner by Baja's unique magic—am humbled by the vastness of its emptiness, the wildness of its waves in winter, the profusion of its stars at night and the magnificence of the gray whales that cruise in front of my house from early winter through spring.

Yes, it's that cool. Want an instant Baja fix? Okay. Get ready to mentally cross the border and get your attitude adjusted. (You know what Jimmy says about how changing your latitude changes your attitude.) To show you what kind of a mental shift you're in for, I'll share with you one of my favorite quotes—from John Steinbeck's book, *The Log of the Sea of Cortez:*

"The very air here is miraculous, and outlines of reality change with the moment. The sky sucks up the land and disgorges it. A dream hangs over the whole region, a brooding kind of hallucination."

Nina, Ann and Victoria on the beach at Puerto Vallarta, 1967

Chilequiles and Our First Mexican Mutt
Christmas Vacation 1967

My mom was a master at what I call culinary plagiarism—especially when traveling. Wherever we went when I was a kid, whenever she tasted something wonderful, she would do her best to sweet-talk the waiter or busboy into giving her the recipe. She was really good at it too, and nearly always succeeded. We'd try the new recipes as soon as we got home. On the few occasions the restaurants wouldn't part with their recipes, Mom would pore through her cookbooks and magazines back home until she found one that was similar. Then we'd hit the kitchen with a vengeance and experiment until we got it just right.

We kept all those recipes in a drawer in the kitchen. Most were Mexican, because that's where we traveled the most. When I got older, my mom handed the recipes on to my sister, Nina and me. We kept up with the culinary plagiarism thing. We got pretty good at it, too, working our way into designated chef status within our circles of friends. When I lived in Colorado in the early '80s, I decided it was time for someone to cook for me once in a while, so I typed up my recipes, xeroxed them and passed them out for Christmas gifts. Over the years, I added more recipes. Then I inserted the stories that went with them, and in 1997, Cooking With Baja Magic was published.

Some of my favorite memories from my teenage years were our holiday trips to Puerto Vallarta, on the Mexican Riviera. It wasn't a world-class resort back then. No American jets landed there. There were no high-rise hotels, discos or fancy restaurants. It was just a sleepy little village by the sea—sultry, warm, deliciously tropical, uncrowded, friendly and exquisitely beautiful. The first year we stayed in a house right on the beach to the north of town, in the middle of what's now "Hotel Row." It was a sprawling house built around a central courtyard. It had tile floors that ended right at the sand and was immaculately furnished with hand-made Mexican furniture. There was a cook who made us breakfast every morning, and a maid to clean up after us. Every day we'd go to Los Muertos Beach just south of the Río Cuale and park ourselves in front of the El Dorado Restaurant—which consisted (and still does) of a palapa-covered patio and some yellow and green *equipale*— pigskin and woven wood—tables and chairs on the sand. I always ordered Chilequiles for lunch. So did my mom and Nina. We ate in our wet bathing suits, right on the sand.

There's one day from that trip that none of us will ever forget. We'd just ordered. My parents were discussing the "Empty Nest Syndrome." I could tell that my dad was worried about my mom being lonely as he anticipated Nina's and my inevitable departure for college. Suddenly he stood up. My eyes followed his until I spotted the cutest little black and white puppy I had ever set eyes on. It was under the pier, on a frayed rope held by one of two little Mexican girls. Within the space of a single minute, my dad bought that dog for $4.00 U.S., plus a few pesos to buy ice cream cones for the little girls. We named her Victoria.

A few minutes later, Victoria fell asleep in Nina's lap. Our lunch arrived and we dug in. A beach vendor selling silver earrings, necklaces and rings diverted Nina's attention. She put her plate on the low table next to her chair and got up to look. When she sat back down, her entire plate of chilequiles was gone. Little Victoria, barely six weeks old, had scarfed the entire meal!

We brought her north with us, in one of Pancho Muñoz' converted World War II cargo planes, across the Gulf of California and up the Baja peninsula, where we landed at the Tijuana airport. Victoria didn't have to fly in the luggage compartment. No way. On that flight she was a regular passenger. Nina and I were the designated flight attendants. While my dad hung out in the cockpit and chatted with Pancho, we delivered sack lunches to the passengers. Victoria trotted behind at our heels.

Once in Tijuana, we picked up our car and headed across the border. It wasn't as easy to bring dogs into the United States back then as it is now. The customs official wasn't sure he should allow our new puppy into the country. We begged. We teared up. We showed him the rabies certificate we'd gotten from a vet in Puerto Vallarta. Eventually, he relented and she made it across, but only after my parents promised to keep her penned up in the yard for six months. Two days later she was in the car, running errands with my mom. Victoria was her shadow for the next 16 years.

At first, Nina and I were jealous of this little Mexican dog. We felt that she'd taken our place as our mom's new, favorite child. But we forgave them both in time. Not so oddly enough, when Terry and I adopted Gonzo and Cassie (our Mexican mutts), Gayle and Derek were jealous too. They felt displaced by our new "babies." Go figure!

Here's a recipe from my cookbook for those Chilequiles that Victoria so coveted. You can eat them for breakfast, lunch or dinner—they're that versatile. This recipe serves six and it will make you think you're right there on the sand, under a palapa, only a few steps away from that 80 degree ocean. Oh yeah! I'm right there with you....

Chilequiles Vallarta

1 1/2 pounds boneless chicken breasts, cooked and cut in chunks
12 corn tortillas
1/2 cup corn oil
2 - 7 ounce cans green chiles, cut in strips
4 cups Chihuahua or Jack cheese, grated
2 cups enchilada sauce (canned is okay)
1 1/2 cups sour cream
2 tbsp milk

Cut tortillas into one inch strips and fry in oil until crisp. Drain on paper towels. Combine enchilada sauce with one cup of sour cream in saucepan. Heat thoroughly.

In a 9 x 11 pan layer the tortilla strips, chicken, chile strips, cheese and enchilada sauce. Repeat. Top with a layer of tortilla strips, sauce and lots of cheese. Bake at 350 degrees for 25 minutes or until cheese is melted and chilequiles are bubbling. Mix milk into remaining half cup of sour cream. Dribble a little over each serving.

Bay of L.A. from the air

Bay of L.A.—Aquarium on the Moon
From the '60s to the '90s

The last time I was in Bahía de los Angeles, or Bay of L.A. as we gringos call it, was in 1990 or 1991. I'd been twice before that with my parents—but not as an "adult." Even though it's been more than a decade since I was there, I can picture the place in my mind as vividly as though it was yesterday. Its primitive, otherworldly beauty impacted me in a way the makes the years and miles melt away.

We were in a motor home that trip. It was early October—too early for most semi-permanent residents to have come back yet. It was hot, and our air conditioner didn't work. Everyone who's driven into Bay of L.A. knows what I'm talking about when I say that your first view of it, after unrelenting miles of parched desert, is a shock. We passed over a rise, and suddenly, out of nowhere, the Gulf leapt up in front of us. The brilliant blue of the water was almost blinding in its intensity. I could've sworn the desert had just heaved itself wide open and given birth to the sea. The contrast of bleached out granite and sandstone mountains against the dancing surface of the Gulf of California made my breath catch in my throat. Pale purple and white islands rose up out of the water and consumed most of the horizon, looking like chunks of the moon that had splashed down to Earth.

We pulled off to the side of the road.

There was a small town toward the south end of the wide bay. Houses and trailers dotted the shoreline in either direction. I squinted against the midday sun. There were at least four pangas fishing off-shore. A lone pickup truck worked its way up a dirt road, a trail of dust chasing it. Suddenly, the whine of an airplane engine burst through the silence. We watched as a single engine plane swooped down and cir-cled, flying low over the ocean. Moments later it landed on a dirt strip near the town.

As we drove through town in search of a good campsite, I noticed that it hadn't changed much since the '60s. Casa Diaz—where we stayed back then, in primitive bungalows right on the beach—was still there, even though Mama and Antero Diaz had both passed away. Back when I was a kid, the only way to reach Bay of L.A. was by air. Little did I know that we were flying with a bona fide Baja legend— Francisco "Pancho" Muñoz. He was a World War II ace who ran Baja Airlines and was a great buddy of my grandfather and Erle Stanley Gardner. Erle loved Bay of L.A. and wrote several books about the place. Pancho still lives there half the year.

His leaflets from those days advertised it as, " ... the Fabulous Fishing Resort in Baja." A flight left Tijuana every Friday morning at 11:00 and returned every Saturday at 2:00 p.m. Round-trip tickets went for $47.52. Flying time was a little over two hours in one of two converted Douglas B-18's (World War II bombers similar to DC-3's). After we'd traveled with Muñoz a few times, he and my dad (who are the same age) became great amigos in their own right.

My memories of those early trips have faded with the years. But I recall long, lazy days swimming, snorkeling and watching the bird and sea life. I remember sunrises that were so beautiful they made my eyes ache. My clearest memory is of a boat trip we took on a barge of some sort, out to the offshore islands—guano-stained white islands inhabited only by birds and other wild creatures adapted to life in a stark, austere environment. We saw sharks. Sea turtles galore. In fact, in those days turtles were so plentiful that turtle jerky, turtle soup and turtle tacos were staples at Mama Diaz' restaurant—along with lobster tacos, enchiladas and tostadas. We saw sea lions, rays ... even a sperm whale. I can still picture the square head, nose and long, long back that seemed to go on forever. It came within about 50 yards of our boat and blew sky high. It rolled in the water, showing us its backside, and then whooshed its tail at us and was gone. Just like that.

I remembered all this as we drove south of town along the road that hugged the shoreline. There were no other cars or campers in sight. We pulled onto a stretch of beach that looked to have been used as a campsite before. There was a fire ring and the ground was hard enough for the motor home. We parked. I got out of to stretch my legs. It had to be well over 100 degrees. The blistering heat wrapped itself tightly around me and threatened to suck my breath away. I had my bathing suit on under my shorts, so I peeled off everything else, ran to the shore, tossed aside my flip-flops and threw myself into the water. It was barely cool enough to be refreshing.

I breast stroked a while, so I could take in the scenery from the water. The offshore islands rose up in front of me like pale ghosts. The surface of the sea was as still as a sheet of blue glass. A flock of sea gulls screeched overhead. From the south came some pelicans, riding the air currents like an invisible roller coaster.

Without warning, less than 50 feet in front of me, the surface of the sea broke. A shiny snub-nosed dolphin arced flawlessly out of the water, through the air and back into the sea—without making a splash. Another followed. Then a third. I swear I was holding my breath. The pelicans began to dive, one by one, sending up huge explosions of white water. The contrast between the pelicans and dolphins made me laugh out loud. The dolphins reminded me of Olympic divers—all smooth fluidity and perfection. The pelicans, on the other hand, were like kids lined up on a diving board, doing cherry bombs into a pool, competing to see who could make the biggest splash.

I swam back to shore. Before I put my feet down, I remembered my mother's warning from 30 years prior, "Shuffle your feet. That will scare the stingrays away." I looked down. Sure enough, a trio of stingrays darted away across the sand like odd-shaped flying saucers with barbed tails. I shuffled my way out of the water.

Nina and Ann with Boys in Baja

Boys 'n Beer in Baja
Easter Break 1969

Unlike my kids, Nina and I loved going camping in Baja and mainland Mexico when we were teenagers. The minute we'd parked and leveled the motor home, rolled out the awning and unloaded the tables, chairs and other gear, we'd grab Victoria, leash her up and tell our parents we were taking her for a walk. What we were really doing, however, was heading off in search of boys. Boys and beer—not necessarily in that order.

We did this every trip. We did it in San Felipe for three Easter vacations. We did it in Guyamas at San Carlos Bay another year. We did it on Memorial Day weekends, again in San Felipe. It was Labor Day weekend just north of Ensenada, where I met Robert, who was to become my boyfriend for my entire senior year of high school. One of my favorite trips was in April 1969. I was 16. Nina was 15. We were camping at Pete's Camp, just north of San Felipe and right on the bluffs above the beach. There was a huge group of us—about seven RVs—clustered together in a circle like a wagon train. There were dune buggies and dirt bikes on the outer rim, along with inner tubes, rafts and the occasional aluminum fishing skiff. ATVs and jet skis hadn't even been invented yet, so things were a bit quieter on the beach and in the water. We had a big fire pit and barbecue in the center of our circle. We shot fireworks off at night on the perimeter while the parents danced inside to the Tijuana Brass.

The Colorado River dead-ends where the Gulf of California begins. About an hour south of the delta is San Felipe, where the low tides are so low you can walk out half a mile across sand and mud flats that were underwater just a few hours earlier. Actually, trudge is more like it. I remember being ankle-deep in mud on my way out to go swimming more than a few times.

The afternoon was hot. San Felipe's climate is similar to that of Palm Springs—only it's on the beach. The tide was almost high, so we could see bait fish jumping and pelicans swooping across the warm ocean, alerting the fleet of panga fishermen and shrimp boats patrolling offshore to the whereabouts of their day's catch.

Feeling a little restless after the five-hour drive, and more than a little bit ready to stir up some action, Nina and I decided it was time to take Victoria for a stroll. It was that magical, mystical time of day right before sunset, when the light is pure gold. We each had a silver ten-peso piece our grandfather had given us for Christmas. We'd been saving them ever since—with boys, beer and Baja in mind.

We wandered down a maze of dirt roads, in search of the cantina. "Where is that cantina?" I asked my sister.

"Right over there." She pointed. We went in and sat down.

"Buenas tardes," I said to the guy who was tending bar. "Dos Carta Blancas, por favor."

We felt mature. Sophisticated. Yet plenty wild too—like authentic, expatriate renegades. He handed us each an ice-cold bottle of beer and we paid up. We were the only customers in the cantina.

A little aside here. When Nina and I lived in Colorado Springs in the early '80s, some friends of ours nicknamed us "Hoover" and "Eureka." Why? Because we could suck down beers faster than most of the guys we knew. You can rest assured we learned (and honed) this skill in the campground cantinas of Baja. After all, we were motivated. We had to down those beers before our parents or any of the other adults in our group showed up and caught us. We learned to drink fast, and we never got caught either!

We drank a beer apiece, and then decided to go looking for boys.

As we scouted the campground, we suddenly heard the roar of an approaching aircraft. We looked up. A single engine plane circled overhead, leveled out for landing and came to a stop on the dirt road right next to us. Mouths hanging wide open, we stared in disbelief as the door to the plane unhinged and out popped a single dad named Steve, his teenage son, Jeff and daughter, Lisa. We waved. They waved. We introduced ourselves. Turned out they were friends of some of the people we were camping with. Nina's eyes lit up. She sidled up to Jeff and started flirting in earnest as we led them to our campsite. By dinnertime they were an item. By 9:00 p.m. they were sneaking off for a kiss or two on the beach. Their romance lasted the entire week—until the little plane took off and faded into the sky.

The day after they showed up, Nina, Jeff, Lisa and I walked out over the mud flats to go swimming. On the way back we stopped in at the cantina. This time it was packed. There were people from our age all the way up to our parents' ages and older. American rock 'n roll was blaring from a jukebox. We sat down and ordered a round of Carta Blancas. The table next to us was all guys—college guys, we soon found out. Within minutes, we'd pushed our two tables together and Lisa and I were set. We were in Baja. We had boys and we had beer. What more could a girl want?

* * * *

Postscript: And Nina and I thought we were wild....

A few days after I wrote this, my dad came to dinner. Historically, getting him to cough up his stories on Baja has been about as easy as getting a cat to follow directions. However, that night he was in an expansive mood. We began reminiscing about this particular trip to San Felipe in 1969. What I didn't know until now was that he and his buddy, Louie Sampo were setting off fireworks one night when we were away from camp. They obviously had a few Margaritas under their belts, because they misfired a skyrocket or two and ended up burning down two palapas on the beach!

Another day on that trip, they went clamming at low tide. Later that night (again after several Margaritas) they cooked the clams in a bucket over the open fire. Everyone gobbled them up. "Best damn clams I ever made," my dad boasted. He chuckled. "Until we got to the bottom of the bucket, that is. There was a solid layer of cigarette butts on the bottom." Yikes. Good thing I didn't eat any....

Sunrise at the Buena Vista Beach Resort, or "Spa"

Buena Vista, BCS—From Here to There and There to Here
June 2001

The air is soft here. The light ripples across the turquoise and azure sea. Tick ... tick ... tick go the sprinklers. Orange lichen creeps across the rooftops, contrasting with the green coconut palms, magenta bougainvillea and yellow hibiscus. The delicate aroma of plumeria blossoms dances across the breeze. The sky is soft too. The puffs of clouds that hid the sun as it rose over the Gulf of California and spread its subtle colors across the bright blue sky—they're gone now.

I snorkeled for an hour this morning before I walked up the road to reward myself with an ice cold Pacifico. I filled our little cooler box with eight, and the guy behind the counter dumped a bag of ice over them. My cooler was heavy walking back down that blistering hot road, but it was worth it. Now Terry can have a chilled beer when he gets back from fishing.

I saw three eels today, a sea turtle and two stingrays, along with the usual bounty of parrotfish, needlefish, pompano, triggerfish and so many others I couldn't begin to name them all. I swam further today than I have before, alone in the sea, delighting in the warm-cool softness of the water, the push-pull of my arms against it, enjoying the tension in my legs as I kicked along. My mask leaked a lot, but it gave me the excuse to stop every so often, to look up at the rugged gray mountains rising up out of the desert to the west of me—stark and adamant against the sea and sky. I thought to myself, "Maybe tomorrow I'll talk Terry into taking a panga down to Cabo Pulmo. The Mexican government has designated the area as an underwater national park. Fishing isn't permitted. Only divers and snorkelers are welcome in the 10 mile long by three-mile wide park covering a coral reef that forms green and rust-colored coral outcroppings that look like huge heads of cauliflower. Yeah, that would be cool....

It was so calm, so peaceful in that water. Every once in a while some gringos would roar by on their four-wheelers, waving—on their way from somewhere to somewhere else. These vehicles—ATVs, quads, four-wheelers, whatever you choose to call them—they're the mode of transportation of choice for the colony of expatriates living here. They're perfect for cruising along the beaches and up in the mountains of the East Cape. I want to live in Mexico, to travel in a motor home to exotic tropical and mountain places, to historic colonial towns. I want to submerge myself in this culture—so simple yet complicated. I want to speak Spanish for days at a time without even knowing I'm doing it. My parents went almost everywhere I long to go, from the early '70s to the early '90s.

We are here right now, in Buena Vista, Baja California Sur—45 minutes north of the Los Cabos airport on the East Cape—one of the premier sport fishing, windsurfing and diving places in the world. This is my father's favorite place on the planet. My mom passed on a couple months ago. He carried her ashes on the plane, in a plain cardboard box inside an ice chest. He brought her death certificate along so that no one would question him. On Sunday we will go out in a boat and spread her ashes with a boatload of Mariachis following behind. There will be nine of us. Dad and Derek flew in on Monday. Today's their third day of fishing. Yesterday Terry and I flew in, got off the plane, collected our bags, passed through customs, had a beer, hit the *caja permanente*—ATM—for pesos and went looking for our ride. I found him bearing a sign that read, "Buena Vista Beach Resort" and said, "Sí, sí." He laughed and replied, "*Ah, la perdida,*" meaning, "the lost one." I guess we'd dawdled a bit. Oh well ... we were already on Mexican time.

This afternoon Nina and her husband, John will arrive, along with Gayle. Our friends, Joe and Marilyn will be here before lunch, as they're flying Aeromexico and the rest of us had chosen to fly Alaska. Odd, isn't it, to fly to hot, sultry southern Baja on a jet with an Eskimo on its tail? I prefer Aeromexico, to be honest. The food's better. There's more legroom and the beer and *bebidas nacionales*—national drinks—

are free.

* * * *

I flew all the way from San Diego to Los Angeles to Hermosillo to Monterrey to Mexico City on April 20th of this year. It took 14 hours to do it—a real milk run. My hotel was nearly an hour from the airport, so by the time I got to bed, it was after midnight. The next day I had to be out in front of my hotel by 7:30 a.m. to catch a flight to Acapulco. All in all, it took me a day and a half to make a trip that would take three hours on a nonstop flight. It was an inordinately difficult trip too. I was exhausted, anxious, worried. My mom was in the hospital when I left. She was dying—we all knew it—but in her moments of lucidity she insisted I make the trip to Acapulco. After all, I was a guest of the Mexican Board of Tourism to Tianguis, their annual tourism convention, as a member of the international press. This was my first invitation, and an incredible honor. I was also scheduled to fly to Guadalajara and then Puerto Vallarta on the 26th. I'd be gone ten days in all.

Early into the convention it became clear that I would have to leave early. There were free phones in the pressroom in Acapulco, and free email too. On the morning of the 24th my dad called me on my cell phone. "Can you get here by tomorrow?" Nina said pretty much the same thing. Terry had flown on American Airlines and I'd flown on Aeromexico. The next day was the end of Tianguis—and everyone in the pressroom assured me I'd never get a flight out. The lady behind the counter told me that my best option would be to take a bus (12 hours) to Mexico City and try to catch a flight north from there. "But there's a nonstop flight from Acapulco to Tijuana," I said. I'd seen it online. "Can't you check that one to see if there's any available seating?"

"No. You have to use the same flights that are on your ticket."

"I can't do that. This is an emergency. Do I have any other options?"

"If you change your flights you'll have to pay."

"I don't care."

She looked at her watch. "Aeromexico opens at 10:00. Third floor of the convention center." It was 9:30.

Leaving Terry outside, I passed through the security check and entered the massive, teeming convention center, using that half hour to check out the exhibits. Tianguis is the eighth largest trade show in the world, and every city, region and major resort in Mexico was represented there. I found the Baja California Sur booth and ran smack into Esaul (pronounced Es-ah-OOL) and Axel Valdez, sons of my dad's longtime *compadre*—especially good friend—Jesus "Chuy" Valdez. I told him I needed to find his dad. "My mom's dying," I said, "and once she moves on, my sister and I will be bringing our dad down to your hotel in Buena Vista." We went every year at least once as a family, from the time Derek was a year old, until four years ago when Mom got sick. It would be Buena Vista, and only Buena Vista that would soothe his heart and ease his grief. We knew this then, and that's why we're here now.

Esaul told me where I could find Chuy later and I went upstairs to Aeromexico. Mexicans, being far more mystically inclined than us gringos, believe in *milagros*—miracles. They adorn handmade crosses with tiny silver and tin symbols of them. A leg, a heart, a flower, a leaf, a cow or horse—all signs of miracles either desired or received. Always on the lookout for milagros, the Mexicans notice them, celebrate them, and thank God when they happen. Thus it was with me that day. I not only ran into old friends, but there was one seat left on the Wednesday nonstop flight from Acapulco to Tijuana, and I got it. Aeromexico even gave me the Tianguis discount, so it ended up costing me very little. I found out later that this nonstop flight was only on Wednesdays and Fridays, so I was triply blessed. The clerk gave me a local toll free number for American Airlines and I headed back to the Press Room to try to change Terry's flight.

That was an even bigger piece of cake. Another milagro. He got seats on the same flights he'd been booked on for Saturday—only on Wednesday. No charge. No fuss. No muss. I called my family. "Terry's flying into San Diego. He gets in a couple hours before me, so he'll pick up his truck, cross back into Mexico and pick me up in Tijuana. I'll call you after I land. By the way, Dad, I found Esaul and I'm gonna go see Chuy in a few minutes. We'll call you." I did find Chuy, finally, and we did call my dad. It was the brightest moment in an otherwise desolate day.

At 1:00 a.m. on Thursday I pulled up to my parents' house. I called Dad from my cell phone. "Damn," he said. "You just made me waste a good $7 sleeping pill. Great to see you though, honey. So glad you made it back." My mom woke up, recognized me from her hospital bed in the den, and then drifted back off with a smile on her face as soon as I told her, "I shook President Fox's hand yesterday!"

We were all there together with her at the end. Now, nearly eight weeks later, we are here in Buena Vista, gathering to honor her, remember her, love her and to cast her earthly remains into the soft, clear waters of the Gulf—a place we all cherish.

* * * *

Last night we had fun. Terry and I partied with Charlie and his buddies Frank and Dick. We met Charlie here about ten years ago. You run into people again and again in a place like this. It's not uncommon. We have an expression in our family that describes what can happen the first night people are gathered together in a resort setting. It's called, "First Night in Camp." What does it mean? Well, it means that people can get a little carried away with whatever they're drinking—be it Margaritas, or cervezas with a side of Hornitos (tequila). Whatever. We had a fairly mild First Night in Camp that night, but while we were at dinner the management moved us to a different hotel room. Apparently, the air conditioning didn't work in ours. I didn't know where our new room was, since I left after Terry because I was looking for the ice machine (gone now, by the way). I got lost. I couldn't find the room. I remembered that it was 27, and wandered around in circles, ending up at room 34 over and over again. I couldn't find 27. The room numbering sequence made no sense at all. No one was awake (fishermen and women go to bed before 10:00 as they're always up at 5:30 or so) except two men sipping Coronas on their patio. I called softly for Terry, starting to panic a little. One of the guys answered me. "I'm Terry. Do I know you?"

Wrong Terry. But he helped me find my room. When my Terry opened the door, I introduced them. "Terry, this is Terry. He heard me calling for you and brought me home." Next morning, I was up before dawn with the fishermen. At the breakfast buffet, the two Terrys had a good laugh at my expense. My First Night in Camp adventure was the talk of the day, and we laughed about it all week. After breakfast, I took pictures of my dad, Terry and Derek heading out to sea in their fishing boat. Then I went back to bed.

This hotel is celebrating its 25th anniversary this year—in October. I remember how it was in the early days. Where my room is now, where the tropical gardens, hand-laid tile pool with its palapa-covered swim-up bar, where the oceanfront dining room and patio is now—all that was one big sandlot. Chuy and his wife, Imelda built this place, *poco a poquito*—bit by tiny bit—over the years. It wasn't "chick friendly" at all in the early days. No way, José. The hotel was mostly populated by huge groups of raucous male fisher-types who partied at least as hard as they fished. The rooms were Spartan and rustic. The showers were iffy. If you got water pressure, often there was only hot water—no cold. That's because the hotel is built over a hot spring. The water has to be cooled, not heated, but it was fun to go swimming in the offshore hot springs at night. The food back then was nothing approaching exotic.

This hotel is now called the Buena Vista Beach Resort, but that's been its name for only about the last five years. Before that, it was Hotel Spa Buena Vista—and everyone who knows it from before still calls it the "Spa." Before it opened, we used to go to Rancho Buena Vista, another fishing resort about a half mile up the beach. Guys like Chuck Connors, Desi Arnaz, Fred Astaire, and Ray Cannon used to hang out there in the '50s and '60s. Back then the waters churned with roosterfish, the wildest fighters in all of the Gulf of California—said to be even more exciting to reel in than a marlin.

The Mexican government is dedicated to preventing this rich sea from being fished dry. Much has been done to eliminate the devastation caused by gill net fishing. A program called *¡Suéltame!* which means "Release Me!" has made it fashionable for fishermen and women to release their big game fish rather than have them stuffed to take home as trophies.

My first time in Buena Vista was Thanksgiving, 1970. I was 18 ... a freshman in college. I was reeling after my first major heartbreak, certain I'd never get past it. "Get over it," my mom clichéed. "There are a million more fish in the sea." I thought her immeasurably cold and hard-hearted back then. Now I know I'd say the same thing to my own daughter—my beautiful, fiery, difficult, opinionated, over-achieving firstborn—Gayle. At 17, she's infinitely more worldly and self-assured than I was as a teenager. Does this make her more or less difficult to live with than Nina and I were? My mom would never tell. She would only laugh and make some remark about me getting my "just desserts."

Derek and Grandpa with his first dorado, 1990

Fishing For Those Little Bastards
May 1991

Derek's first trip to Baja was in May of 1987. He wasn't born yet, but he was definitely there in my very pregnant (as in seven months pregnant) belly. When he was a year old, we camped south of La Misión. While Gayle went horseback riding, he hung out in his playpen or went for beach walks in a backpack. Since then, we've done plenty of airplane trips and camping trips to Baja, with even more weekend trips and vacations to La Bufadora.

Derek's first really big, supremely exciting trip to Baja took place in 1991, when he was not quite four. This was the first time he was old enough to go fishing alone with his grandpa. We went, of course, to the Spa.

Since I have one sister and no brothers, my dad—passionate fisherman that he is—never had a son to fish with. He over-fished Nina and me before we were out of grade school. After that, we'd snorkel, but fishing? No gracias. The poor guy was devastated that we failed to fall in love with his favorite sport. Dad never had a bona fide fishing buddy in the family until Derek. He took a photo of Derek with his first big Dorado and used it as his company Christmas card that year. And Derek is really and truly a fisherman. For years, he suffered from seasickness. Did it faze him? Not a bit. He always told me he felt just fine as soon as he barfed. In the summer of 2001, he caught a 302-pound marlin. He loves to fish with a passion that equals that of his grandpa.

Anyway, at lunch the day after Derek caught his first Dorado, my mom and I were quizzing him about the day. "Well, it was kind of boring after we caught my Dorado. All we caught were a couple of little bastards, and we had to throw them back," he explained in a serious, matter-of-fact voice.

Silence reigned around the table. Eyebrows were reaching for the ceiling. My dad walked into the dining room and sat down. "Togo. Did you swear in front of your grandson?" my mother asked, her voice dripping icicles.

His eyes widened. "What? Me? Of course not," he said. He was all innocence.

"You didn't call some fish 'little bastards' out on the boat?" she asked. My sister and I looked at each other, grabbed our napkins, covered our mouths and tried to stifle our laughter. Derek looked from me to Nina in confusion.

"What did I say wrong?" Derek asked. I leaned over and whispered in his ear. "Oh," he said, his eyes as big as saucers. "But Nonnie, I thought little bastards were a type of fish. I didn't know Grandpa was saying bad words."

From that day on, whenever our family gets together, Derek and Nina vie for story-telling rights on the infamous fish story. No matter where we are, all one of them has to do is say, "Hey, Derek ... " (Or "Hey, Nina.... ") "Remember those L.B.s?"And we all crack up.

Derek, Gayle and fireworks

Fourth of July in Baja
1962 and Onward

I remember the first Fourth of July I spent in Baja. I was nine. My parents and three other families rented cute little houses called casitas at Quintas Papagayo Resort, just north of Ensenada, for a week. There were a dozen kids from ages five to twelve and we had free run of the place from sunup 'til bedtime. We spent as many hours a day as we could in the pool or hunting sea creatures in the tide pools along the shore. We had big barbecues every night. We drove into town and searched the shops for silver jewelry, *huaraches*—Mexican sandals, blouses and colorful pieces of folk art. Our favorite purchase of all was fireworks. After all, this was the season for skyrockets, Roman candles, sparklers, poppers, cherry bombs, M-80s and plain old fireworks—the louder the better. We loaded up.

After we finished shopping, the moms and kids ate lunch at a little place next door to Hussongs while the dads had a few cervezas in the bar. I remember trying to peer around the corner of those mysterious green doors and see inside the famous (or infamous, depending on your point of view) cantina that had been around since before the turn of the century. There was no way the doorman would let me do it, though. I had to wait 'til I turned 18 before I was allowed inside. The first time I had a beer with my dad in Hussongs was the day before his 79th birthday.

Anyway, Fourth of July in Baja always starts a few days ahead of time. After all, with all those fireworks stashed in everyone's cars, hotel rooms, tents and RVs, the temptation to light a few off as soon as the sun goes down is overwhelming. I noticed that big time the year I was camping out at Agua Caliente in Punta Banda, where Terry has a bachelor pad. Fourth of July was on a Sunday that year, and most people had Monday off—so this was a serious three-day-weekend.

It was packed, toe-to-toe. The campgrounds were full of big groups of Mexicans and Americans camping side by side. There were jet skis zooming around in the water all day long, winding their way between boogie-boarders, surf-kayakers and swimmers. There are geothermal springs offshore. At low tide you can dig a hole in the sand, right at the shoreline and make your own hot tub right on the beach. The water is scalding, and unless you let in a little seawater when a wave comes, it's too hot to sit in for very long. There were vendors cruising the beach selling jewelry, fruit, fresh fish on skewers, sodas and toys. Down at La Jolla Camp they sold tacos, hot dogs and other goodies. For a few dollars, girls and a few daring guys, could get their hair braided into cornrows ornamented with fluorescent plastic beads. There were bocce ball tournaments, volleyball games and more dogs than you can imagine. In the distance I could see four-wheelers roaring up the beach and horses plodding along at a much more leisurely pace. It was fiesta time at *la playa*—the beach—that was for sure.

There were firecrackers going off all day long, beginning on Friday. By the time evening rolled around the Roman candles and fancy, multi-colored fireworks came out. Roman candles look like flares. They shoot up a few hundred feet in the air and explode into pink balls, with wakes of light streaming behind them. There are bigger fireworks, more typical of what we have in the U.S.A. too, but most folks save these for the real event.

Snugs, my dog, was one of those canines who freak out at loud noises. After the first pop on Friday, he was curled into a tiny ball, wedged into a corner of Terry's cabaña, shivering and trying his best to disappear. Sadly, he pretty much stayed there for the next three days. On Sunday, as soon as the sunset, my group joined the hordes out on the seawall. There were hundreds of people, and everybody had their own stash of pyrotechnics. Derek and friends were beside themselves with excitement and anticipation. "Can we start yet, Mom? Can we? Can we?" he asked over and over again. Luckily he had some sparklers, those hand-held things that flare up like exploding stars. I remembered those from when I was his age and asked him to let me light one off. I waved it around in the air like a magic wand, loving the shooting and trailing sparks as much as I had as a kid.

I've seen magnificently orchestrated and choreographed Fourth of July shows, but nothing that could compare to that year's experience. It was mayhem. There were no real rules; no one was in charge, yet somehow it all seemed to flow together perfectly—in a freewheeling, wild and wacky sort of way. The night was clear, but the air over the beach was thick with billowing smoke. Mexican ranchero music competed with rock 'n roll music in both English and Spanish. The sounds of laughter were everywhere. The explosions and light show lasted for nearly two hours, until everyone ran out of things to light off. Slowly the crowd dissipated and everyone went back to their campsites to have another cerveza around the campfire and relive the whole thing ... once ... twice ... and then ... one last time ... until the next year!

Part Two: Tales from La Bufadora

Terry blowing the conch shell at sunset. A La Buf ritual.

Getting Boofed in La Bufadora
Memorial Day Weekend 1994

La Bufadora you've got my soul;
your waves crash through my mind.
No lights ... no locks ... no phone ... no mail
not even smoke-free dining.
Your rules are etched upon brown hills.
Unspoken code of ethics.

It's a safe harbor for our hearts.
No fears ... no tears ... no lying.
A magic cove perched all alone.
A place knocked out of time.

Several mornings a week about 10:00 a.m., the buses begin their descent from the crest of Punta Banda into the village of La Bufadora. They disgorge crowd after crowd of tourists who swarm the "Mall," a row of shops lining the roadway to La Bufadora, or the Blow Hole—one of Mexico's most visited natural wonders. American and Mexican visitors alike bargain with local shopkeepers for silver jewelry, folk art, *curios*—souvenirs, blankets, clothes, hammocks, sunglasses and leather goods. They munch on tacos, *churros*—cinnamon-coated donuts, and chile-sprinkled mangos as they work their way out to the Blow Hole, where—if they're lucky—they'll get drenched by one of its roaring blows.

The name La Bufadora actually comes from the verb *bufar*, which means to snort, so the literal translation is, "The Snorter." And it does snort, believe me, as the sea is sucked into an underwater cave and erupts into the air. The first time I visited here was back in the mid-'70s. The only things around then were a couple of outdoor restaurants with rusty metal tables and creaky, folding chairs, lots of flies and a precarious, slippery path that led right down to the water spout. Things have changed a lot since then. With the Mall's renovation a few years ago, and the addition of electricity soon after, the place is able to offer a lot more to tourists than it did before. Yet, somehow, it still has the flavor and feeling of the Mexico I grew up loving as a child, and missed until I rediscovered La Buf on Memorial Day weekend in 1994.

To gringos like me, who have second homes and trailers at Rancho La Bufadora (a private ranch surrounding *Bahía Papalote*—Butterfly Bay) it's a whole different world—a remote, old-style paradise only two hours south of the border. Everywhere between here and there is full of Americanized hotels charging Americanized prices. Here, there are a few houses and trailers to rent that you can ferret out, but there's no hotel. Most visitors never get any further south than the outdoor deck of one of the many restaurants and taco stands. Let me take you along on a tour....

After you board your tour bus (or point your car south) to La

Bufadora, prepare to be awestruck by the beauty that surprises you en
route. Heading out of Ensenada, you'll see groves of olive trees, fields
of artichokes, chiles, lettuce and vibrant purple, fuchsia and yellow
flowers as you pass through Maneadero and turn right onto a country
road. Going west on BC 23 toward the *cerro*—peak—that crowns
Punta Banda-Banded Point, you'll see more fields and livestock. The
impressive, multi-hued Cerro Ramajal Mountains to the south, the
crisp blue of the ocean and the winding waterways amid the rushes of
the *estero*—estuary—will take your breath away. After you bounce
over the last *tope*—speed bump—just past the town of Punta Banda,
the road snakes along cliffs at the edge of Bahía Todos Santos. The
view of Ensenada from here is the best there is. If you came on a
cruise ship, you'll see it waiting at anchor below the huge Mexican
flag on the *malecón*—waterfront boardwalk. If you're making the drive
during the late winter or early spring—look out for migrating gray
whales spouting in the turquoise waters below you.

    As you begin your descent into La Bufadora, look to the
south. See all the little houses and trailers dotting the hillside around
the bay? The Blow Hole is down the road to your right. The houses are
all on private land owned by the Toscano family of Ensenada. Our
patrón is renowned Mexican political satirist and long-time PAN sup-
porter (PAN rose to the forefront in Mexico in July, 2000 when
Vicente Fox won the presidency and ended the PRI's 71-year reign of
power), José León Toscano—a.k.a "El Tigre." He's over 80—but he's
still vital, and he loves his rancho. Once you park and finish checking
out the shops and the Blow Hole, take a few minutes to sit down at
one of the ocean-view restaurants. Order yourself an ice-cold cerveza
and look out across the bay.

    See the water sparkle as sunrays dance across its surface?
Notice how its depth and clarity are revealed by the aquamarine color,
accented with cobalt blue? See trails of bubbles rising up from divers
exploring the depths below? Whoa! Wasn't that a seal whose head just
popped up through the kelp, surprising a pair of kayakers on their way
out to the Blow Hole? See the squadron of pelicans circling the cliffs
in formation, and then dive-bombing into the water to scoop up lunch?
The craggy terrain may remind you of Greece; the shoreline, for me,
also conjures up visions of Big Sur. Are you beginning to get a little
more curious about those colorful houses dotting the hillside?

    See that dust-covered four-by-four truck heading up the road?

Wonder where he's going? Your eyes follow the cloud of dust until it disappears behind the top row of houses hanging over the edge of the bay, and then reappears briefly, only to disappear again behind a knoll. You see a propane truck winding its way up the hill, honking its horn intermittently. A big black and white truck with "Tony Sanchez" written on its doors lumbers by, liquid sloshing from its rear as it too grinds its way up, bringing water to the houses on the hill.

Unless you know someone who has a casa in Rancho La Bufadora, or unless you're a tough sort who doesn't mind camping in the dirt, you probably won't experience this side of La Buf firsthand. You'll just soak up the beauty, finish your beer, snap a few pictures and climb back into your car or tour bus. But—if curiosity gets the better of you, and if you start feeling a little tingling in your soul— well, you may be well on your way to getting, as we say in La Bufadora—"boofed." That's what happened to me. Nina and John invited me, a friend and her kids to stay in a rental house for the long weekend. As I ate a $1.40 breakfast on the patio of Los Gordos, I watched the scene described above unfold before me. It was beautiful, peaceful, festive, lonely, comforting and magical. My heart stirred, my eyes misted up and in an inexplicable way, I felt I'd come home. Oh yes. I was "boofed!"

One characteristic common to people who visit La Buf is a tendency to stay at least one extra day. We did, and we came back again, again and again that summer. Like a magnet, La Bufadora kept drawing me back. My buddy Jim has a saying: "The more you go to La Bufadora ... the more you go to La Bufadora." That pretty much sums it up. The raw remoteness of the place sets it apart from the frenzied, chaotic motion of Southern California. Being there relaxed me, right down to the nitty-gritty nooks and crannies of my being. It took me back to an earlier, simpler time when a handshake sealed a deal and people looked out for one other. It epitomized the Baja I'd come to cherish as a child—a Baja I couldn't find anywhere else that wasn't at least a 12-hour drive away.

Nina and I ended up buying a house together at the end of that summer. We had to. We'd exhausted all of our houseguest possibilities and had to find a place of our own.

Ann's van and the water truck

Dirt Roads in the Dark
Winter 1995

The first night I ever spent in La Bufadora, the kids and I decided to walk from Gordos to the house we were renting. Kathy took my van and said she'd meet us later. It was a dark, moonless night. There was no electricity, so there were no lights. None of us had a flashlight. All the roads are still dirt, and all of them meander around in a semi-meaningless way.

We made it past Dale's Dive Shack. I thought I saw a shortcut, and motioned the kids to follow me. All of a sudden there was no road under my feet. I slipped, and slid on my backside down a short but gravelly incline. Getting up and dusting myself off, I continued onward. We went across an expanse of open ground and into some trees.

"Which way do we go now?" Gayle asked. There were three or four choices. I heard strains of some Jimmy Buffett music off to my left.

"Let's go that way." We went a little further, made a couple more turns, trying to locate the source of the music. We couldn't, and after about 15 minutes of wandering around in circles, we gave up.

"Do you think we can find our way back to Gordos?" the kids

asked. I hoped so.

We made it back to the dive shack and encountered Kathy, Nina and John in my van. Thankfully, my sister knew her way back to the house we were staying in. As we wound our way through the maze of dirt roads, I was astounded. It had all looked so easy in the daylight. But in the near-total darkness, I was utterly clueless as to where we were going. I just knew that we could've traipsed around all night and never made it home.

After Nina and I bought our house, I still had problems negotiating the roads at night. It took a couple of years before I really knew my way around. That first winter, after our "Friday Nights at Gordos," we'd always head over to Dick and Vee's house where Dick would play his guitar and we'd all sing old rock 'n roll songs off key. As the crows flew, their house was due north of us, in a straight line and at the same elevation. However, there were at least four or five different ways to get from Point A to Point B and I never took the same road home twice.

One trip, in February of 1995, Nina and I came down alone. We'd left after work, so it was dark when we arrived. Rather than going to the house and unloading, we went straight to Gordos. We were starving and craving tacos. It was a busy night. Of course, it's always busy at Gordos on a Friday night. It was after 11:00 when we headed home after stopping at Dick and Vee's.

"Do you know where you're going?" Nina asked me.

"More or less. Well, no. Not really. But I always get home eventually. It's fun. Just think of it as an adventure."

We wound our way up and down and around and finally got to the bottom of our driveway. I turned left to go up. All of a sudden, the van lurched forward and pitched down with a huge thump.

"What was that?" we asked simultaneously. I tried the gas pedal. It whirred. The tires spun. I wasn't going anywhere. I was stuck.

We got out to look. "Oh shit," I said. "The front tire's in a ravine. I swear, that ravine was not there when I was here the last time."

"Well, it did rain," Nina reminded me. Just then we saw headlights. "Oh good," she said. "Maybe whoever this is can pull us out."

It was Manny, husband of Celia, who runs one of the Boof restaurants. He pulled up next to us. "We're stuck," I told him.

He shook his head and laughed. "That's obvious. Had a bit to drink, did you? Well, go to bed. Your car's not going anywhere tonight."

Not inebriated, but thoroughly embarrassed, we grabbed our suitcases and hiked up the driveway, cursing ourselves for forgetting to bring flashlights. We unlocked the house, turned on the (dim) solar lights and dutifully went to bed.

Next morning we were the talk of La Buf. Vee came by with her camera to record my misadventure for posterity. Milo came by. Miguel Toscano came by, driving his water truck.

"I can pull you out," he said. He and Milo hooked a chain from his back bumper to my back bumper. Within minutes, my van was free. And amazingly, it was undamaged. He wouldn't let me pay him either. As he drove away, he smiled and said, "Have a La Bufadora day."

The moral of this story is: Do not assume you know your way in the dark on dirt roads after it rains—especially after a Friday Night at Gordos. Oh, and keep a flashlight in the car at all times.

Susie, courtesy of Jerry Snow

Susie the Camp Dog Spills the Beans

"Hey there. My name is Susie. I'm nine years old and I've lived in La Bufadora most of my life. I'm about 45 pounds of pure scratchy, scraggly, smelly, dirty brownish-black mutt ... and I'm darn proud of it. I'm popular around Rancho La Bufadora because I'm more elusive and fickle than a cat. Everyone loves me ... well, most of them do. Everyone knows me, that's for sure. If you want me to hang around your house, my rules are few and they're simple. Basically, feed me. Steak, fish and chicken scraps are preferred. Dog food ... nah. Not if you have something better. Do not attempt to bathe me. I will leave. Same with brushing. I prefer dog-free places to homes with annoying, barking dogs who get all the best scraps.

"It all began for me here back in about '95 when some Bozo (my former owner) decided to ditch me. He drove to the far end of camp in the middle of the night. He let me out and beat feet. He drove like a bat out of hell, going so fast and stirring up such a cloud of dirt that I didn't have a hope of catching him. I chased him as far as the office, and then lost him. I was out of breath and panting hard so I had to rest and get my bearings. I sniffed around. Hmm, maybe this place wasn't so bad after all. It sure had to be better than being tied up day and night. I was free. My collar was gone too. I sniffed some more. I began to get excited. There were lots of other dogs here. Guinea hens too. Better stay away from them; I'd seen dogs shot for lesser sins than killing and eating a guinea hen. I wondered if there would be any male dogs to hang with. The jerk who ditched me on the side of the road had at least been responsible enough to have me spayed, so I didn't have to worry about birth control. Yeah ... life could be worse!

"The first person I hooked up with was John Savage. He was a nice old dude who has since moved on to more heavenly pastures. I hung with him for a while. There were a bunch of firemen just up from his house. I visited them when they were in town, always hanging low and off to the side. They barbecued a lot and had some darned good leftovers. Steak bones. Rib bones. Oh yeah. I wonder when they're coming back? I can taste that meat already. But then, Jim and Lois are good for bones too, and they always bring down my all-time favorite treat—Lorna Doons! In fact, they haven't been down for a couple of weeks. I bet they'll be here any day now. Better go check it out....

"My longest stint at any one house was with Pam and Gene. Gene's gone now too, but when he was around he was one okay guy ... most of the time. I lived with them for about two years. I stood guard every night. Since they have the hugest house on the ranch, I worried about them. It's an awfully conspicuous house, and Gene had a veritable construction yard on the lower level. Lots of valuable stuff ... even a backhoe. I certainly didn't want anyone trying to rip him off. Pam did a bad thing once, but I forgave her. She threw me into the back of the truck and hauled me to the vet for shots. What a stressful ride! I was just sure she was gonna ditch me somewhere in the middle of the night and I'd have to give up my cushy life. But she didn't. She brought me home and fed me good stuff. So I let her off the hook.

"I used to love chasing Gene's truck. I'd follow him wherever he went on the ranch, but never any further. Nope. This is my place and I'm sticking to it. I loved hanging out waiting for him while he was at Gordos. Of course, I always preferred it when he brought treats with him when he came out. What ruined everything though was when he built me a darned doghouse. Me? A free spirit, held captive at night! The outrage of it all! So what if it was a fancy doggy condo with portholes in it. No way, José. I was outta there the next morning.

"I lived with Jerry for a while ... until he ran over me, that is. We were well suited to one another ... both minding our own business. He didn't try to domesticate me, bathe me or make me a house pet. He liked me just the way I was. Too bad he didn't drive so well....

"Nowadays, I have a new outlook on life. Instead of just hanging around napping all day and sniffing out goodies around sunset, I have a job. I am a 'Trash Dog.' My buddy, Pinto and I, get to run around behind the trash truck all day long. We get great exercise and we get to do equally great trashcan diving. You wouldn't believe some of the incredible food some of the gringos around here throw away. Things like cake, leftover meat, cheese, eggs, crackers, chips, and cookies. We eat like a king and queen on our trash runs. It's light years better than raw mussels, which is what I've had to rustle up on the beach when there's no one around. And, I don't have to worry about being bathed or brushed.

"So that's my story, and I'm sticking to it. Yes ... well I did kill those kittens one night. I didn't mean to. I thought they were doggie chew toys. I wasn't very popular for that move and had to lay low for a day or so. I still don't think Amy has forgiven me. Neither has Jim, for that matter. Other than that, I'm good to go. I don't offend (unless you find my odor noxious) and I am very pleased to be the La Bufadora Camp Trash Dog."

Jerry and Vee loading up the kayaks

As the Boof Blows—Kayaking Adventures
Summer and Fall 1995

One Friday night at Gordos during the summer of 1995, Jerry approached me and asked if I'd like to kayak all the way around Punta Banda the next morning. Hey, why not? We knew we could only make the trip one way, as it would take three or four hours, so we made arrangements with Vee and Dinorah to pick us up on the north side of Punta Banda, near Campo Arnaiz.

Jerry picked me up at 8:00 a.m. and we loaded my kayak next to his on top of the camper shell on his truck. We drove to the launch ramp by the dive shack and headed out. It was July, but you wouldn't have guessed it by the weather. It was cold. Damp. Foggy. We both had on shorts, t-shirts and sweatshirts. We had water and snacks. Jerry, a professional photographer (whose work graces most of the postcards on the market featuring La Bufadora) brought along his camera. He packed it in a plastic bag and carefully stowed it in a watertight compartment.

We paddled out of Bahía Papalote, past the Blow Hole, waving to the vendors on the mall as they laid out their goods in anticipation of the busloads of tourists that would show up around ten. We saw a couple of good blows and turned the corner to the north. Two panga-loads of divers motored past us, waving. They were headed for the "Pinnacles," guano-covered rocks that jut up out of the water around the corner, to the north of the point. We paddled through and around the Pinnacles ... stopping every so often so that Jerry could take pictures.

It was rough out there. I was watching him, talking, gesturing and not paying attention to what I was doing. I gestured myself off balance. My kayak lurched to the left and I was upside down—overboard—in the frigid water, before I knew what had happened! My paddle floated one way, my flip-flops another. My water bottle was bobbing between them. My granola bars were nowhere in sight. I grabbed my boat, turned it right side up and dog-paddled around, gathering up my stuff. Luckily, the summer before, I'd taught myself how to remount a kayak from the water, without falling in again. I jumped up and threw myself flat on my stomach; face forward on top of the boat. Then I lifted myself up, straddled it and pulled myself into a sitting position. I did it right on the first try, thank God. I was okay, but I was wet and freezing, and it we were only about 30 minutes into our adventure. Long way to go....

Five minutes later, Jerry took some more photos. He put his camera back in the hold and turned to me. "God, these are gonna be some great photos," he said. "I can't believe how cool I am." He gestured toward me with his paddle and was instantly upside down. Laughing so hard I almost fell out again myself, I paddled over and helped him retrieve his gear. He was laughing so hard that it took him a couple of tries to get back on his boat.

"Talk about instant karma," he said. "I guess I'm not so cool after all." Then he checked to make sure his camera was okay. It was, but we were both freezing. We hadn't thought to bring extra clothes, and it didn't look as though the sun was going to come out anytime soon.

We paddled on. We paddled for another three hours and the sun never did come out until right before we landed at Campo Arnaiz. By then we were practically dry. I hadn't realized until that day how little of Punta Banda is actually accessible from the road. This is wild terrain—fog enshrouded much of the year. Even in July, it was covered in a green mossy kind of grass that reminded us of Ireland. We saw a house we didn't know existed. It was huge—a mansion more accurately, and perched atop a steep cliff overlooking a perfect, secluded beach.

We kept paddling ... past Rancho Packard and finally on toward Arnaiz. By then, all we could talk about was beer. Why hadn't we brought any? If we ever did this again, we would definitely pack a cooler. Would Vee and Dinorah think to bring beer ... and what about food? We were hungry and our snacks were on the bottom of the ocean.

Finally, the launch ramp at Arnaiz came into sight. Vee's red Blazer was there, and she and Dinorah were waiting for us, waving from the shore. And yes, that was a cooler of beer we saw next to the car. Hallelujah!

* * * *

We made other trips, but none that long. Once, that fall, we kayaked with Jim and John and Nina to "Long Beach"—a secret surf spot around the corner to the south of Bahía Papalote. Jim's wife, Sue walked with the kids and dogs. I much prefer to make this trip by sea. The journey on foot takes almost an hour, and the last leg is straight down a cliff. How surfers zip down that precipice—wearing flip-flops and holding onto their boards—is beyond me. Sue had found an alternate route on an earlier trip—one where you slide down a dirt pile for about a hundred yards on your butt. That was a far superior way to descend, in my opinion—even if you did end up dirty.

Anyway, we paddled to Long Beach, stopping at "Crocodile Rock" for a quick snorkel. The water wasn't terribly cold that day. Usually, the ocean near La Buf is in the high 50s to low 60s in the summer—and it isn't usually swim or snorkel-friendly—not without a wetsuit. We got to Long Beach and rode the waves into shore. The kids, Sue and I took the boats out. We parked on the largest of the two rock islands off shore, jumped overboard and snorkeled some more. We were better prepared this time. It was a warm day. No one fell out of their boat and we'd remembered to pack plenty of snacks and beer. After a picnic, we headed back the way we came.

The Boof Beach

It All Happened at the Boof Beach Club

Jerry has a saying that we, in La Bufadora, are a volunteer community. We aren't there because of a job or family connections. We're there because we want to be. We come for ocean views, the fresh air, the freedom ... and we drive anywhere from two and a half to twelve hours just to get there. We pretty much all know each other in La Buf. By the way, if you're wondering why I alternate between "La Buf" and "the Boof"—it's because the first is the Spanish spelling and the second is the English. If you say "la," you spell it the Spanish way—La Buf. If you say "the," you spell it the English way, the Boof.

When you drive into La Buf, you can't see the beach. It's there, below a cluster of homes in what's called, "Shit Hole Hollow." It's anything but shitty—being right on the beach and all. You have to wind your way between houses, down stairs and across a vacant lot (full of vehicles on hot summer days) to get to another set of stairs that ends on an empty concrete slab. This slab overlooks the sand, which is accessible by yet another stairway. This slab is the home of "La Bufadora Beach Club."

We don't pay dues at this club. Automatic membership is one of the perks of living here. We have umbrellas and rusted but useable beach chairs. We share these. We have a fleet of kayaks, all padlocked together. We bring our paddles with us and share the combination. We bring coolers, magazines, beach towels and dogs (La Buf is a leash-free zone) and set up camp on the slab. If the weather is really warm we bring other beach toys, like inner tubes and rafts. The water's cold, but it's clear and the bay is deep. That makes it great for diving and snorkeling. Spear fishing and kayak fishing too. There are too many people in the water, and the bay is too small to be safe for jet skis. We discourage them mightily, but fortunately they don't show up too often—only on the hottest days of summer.

Obviously, the holiday weekends are the busiest. I remember one Labor Day weekend. The weather was perfect. The ocean was almost 70 degrees—a miracle in and of itself. Jack and Ardell and Pat and Jeff were down. All the firemen were there. Jim and Sue were there, Cathy, John and pretty much everyone else in our age group that has a place there. It was too hot to sit on the slab, so we put our chairs at the water's edge so the waves would cool our toes. There were 12 or 15 kayaks on the beach, nearly all of them in use at any given moment. Marc went out on one, turned it upside down and stood on his head. He had on flesh-colored trunks that made him look naked from afar. All the kids grabbed boats, followed him out into the bay, turned their boats upside down and started gallivanting in the waves, diving, screaming and laughing.

My neighbor Kathy was visiting, and determined to learn to kayak. I led her out through the waves, helped her get in a boat and handed her a paddle. She touched her paddle to the water, lurched and flipped over. I got her in again. She flipped over. After the fourth try, Phil swam over. He had her balanced within two minutes, and we were paddling out toward the Blow Hole, waving at the tourists who gawked at us from above.

Later on, as the sun was close to setting and the sky was turning gold, Sue grabbed her Hawaiian sling and facemask and headed into the ocean, hunting for halibut. Nina and I followed her, but mask-free. We swam to the boats and back. When I go out there, I prefer not to see what's underneath me. I'm weird that way. When I'm snorkeling, I go slow and look around, but when I swim to the boats, I'm jammin' and I don't look down. My sister's the same way. As we were headed back to shore that day, we heard Sue yelling and saw her motioning to us. We swam over to her. She had speared what had to be a 30-inch halibut. She hauled it to shore and everyone crowded around her to check it out.

"John!" Nina called. "Get your sling and get out there!"

* * * *

There's a parking lot of sorts above the Beach Club. On a summer day, it gets crowded and it's a bit tricky getting in and out on the skinny piece of pavement that hangs precariously over a deep gulch. One summer, over Fourth of July weekend (a very busy weekend, of course) I was riding home from the beach with Jerry in his pickup. He was expounding on some subject or the other while driving up this little piece of road. I was facing him, listening. All of a sudden, there was a big thunk and a clunk on my side of the truck. We tilted off toward the gully and down, and then stopped.

"Oh shit," he said. We were listing to the right.

"What happened?"

"Don't get out yet. I think the front tire went over the edge." We carefully climbed out his side of the truck and he went up to Pam and Gene's to look for Gene. Only Gene's backhoe could remedy this situation.

I went back down to the Beach Club. There had to be 25 or 30 people there. Within five minutes, everyone was up on the road checking out Jerry's faux pax. We heard the rumble of Gene's backhoe as it came lurching down the road. Jerry followed, looking like he wished he was anywhere else but there.

"Did you have to tell everyone?" he whispered.

I laughed 'til my sides ached. The cameras came out en masse and his predicament was recorded for posterity. Gene drove his big old backhoe down the road with practiced ease, beer in hand, grinning and waving at the crowd. Guys rushed forward to help him attach the bucket to Jerry's bumper, and within a few minutes, the truck was rescued. But the story lives on....

* * * *

Another time, during President's weekend a few years back, my friend Tom and I went kayaking. We were at the south edge of the bay, right under what is now my house. All of a sudden he yelled and started paddling like crazy. He stopped and started tapping the side of his boat. A head came up to take a peek. It was a baby gray whale. I freaked and back-paddled like crazy. It was a hot day, but the water was icy and I didn't want to be upended by a whale. He kept tapping. Fifty feet to my right came a blow, then a flash of backside and a tail. The baby came up again to spyhop right next to Tom. Then the mom did. They were closer now. I looked to shore. Was there anyone around to witness this spectacle? Would anyone believe us if we told them what happened? Our whale encounter lasted about five minutes, and then the momma and baby turned right and headed north, out of the bay.

We beached our kayaks and walked to Gordos for breakfast. Cathy was out on the patio with some friends. We had witnesses....

Ann and Snugs kayaking at the Blow Hole

Snugs—The Kayaking (Autistic?) Wonder Dog
1995

I once had a very unusual dog. His name was Snugs and we figured he was a cross between a collie and a golden retriever, with a little borzoi thrown in to keep him from ever getting middle-aged spread. The kids and I adopted him knowing he was emotionally challenged, but we loved him anyway. He cringed. He cowered. Loud noises sent him diving into the nearest corner, where he'd curl himself into a tight little ball and shiver. Firecrackers were his worst nightmare, but he got almost as panic-stricken by the Goodyear (or any other) blimp. He didn't fetch, bark at burglars (we got robbed once and he just sat there) and sometimes when he was seriously stressed he wouldn't eat for days.

Looking into his eyes, even then, when he was only six months old, was fairly disconcerting. There was a sadness, a depth and sensitivity in them that you wouldn't expect to see in a dog. It was like he was a human trapped in a dog's body.

Snugs had been aptly named by his first owners. He was the most snuggly dog I've ever known. If a group of people was sitting or standing around, he'd come up to someone and lean his nose against one of their thighs. Invariably he would get plenty of pets that way. Everyone who knew him (unless they weren't dog people) adored him. His specialness was so clearly obvious. People sensed his fragility too. There was something about Snugs that made you want to protect him.

Derek and Snugs bonded big time. That bond never faltered, but grew stronger as the years passed. He slept on Derek's bed every night for eleven years. He didn't just curl up by my son's feet—he slept with him—spoon-style. Back when he was still in diapers, Derek would climb onto Snugs' back and take his afternoon nap on top of him—both of them on the sofa.

Snugs would howl at the door and bark if we left him outside. This was the only time he barked. In his younger days, he'd climb over the fence like a cat to get out of the yard—like I'd imprisoned him or something. I'd pull into the driveway and he'd slink out from under a bush where he'd been napping—stretching and wagging his tail at me, while giving me one of those slightly ticked off and disappointed looks that made it abundantly clear I'd done him wrong. I remember one time I accidentally shut him in my closet. My neighbor, Kathy and I called and called for him. When we couldn't find him anywhere, we scoured the neighborhood. We made flyers and put them on every telephone pole. My folks came over and helped in the search. By the time Gayle and Derek came back from their dad's, we were pretty much sure he was gone for good. I told Gayle. She burst into tears. A moment later we heard a bark. She ran into my room, flung the closet door open and threw herself on the dog. He ran downstairs, out the front door and lifted his leg on a tree—for a very long time.

We've taken countless trips to Mexico—just Snugs and I in the van. He rode shotgun. In fact, in all those years, I never went anywhere without him unless he was plain old not invited. He never stayed in a kennel. He "visited" friends and family, but I would never have dared institutionalize him. He was way, way too sensitive to be locked up again.

That brings me to the kayaking part. It all started one day on the beach at La Bufadora. It was late summer. The morning dawned hot and mostly sunny, except for a few wispy ribbon clouds that hung over the mountaintop. The humidity was down and the Santa Ana winds were blowing. It promised to be a perfect beach day. Gayle, Derek and I were anxious to try out the new sea kayaks I'd gotten for my birthday. We loaded them into the van, packed up our beach gear and cooler, called for Snugs and took off.

We launched the boats, one by one. Gayle got in one and Derek crouched behind me in the other. We paddled off. Thirty seconds later the howling began. I turned my kayak around and grimaced. Snugs stood in the shallow water, wailing as pitifully as if he'd been abandoned for good. I came close to shore and tried to reason with him. Some people on the beach tried to distract him. No luck. He wouldn't shut up and he wouldn't budge. He wasn't about to let us strand him there on the beach. We paddled back and beached our boats, wondering what in the world to do next.

"Mom," said Gayle. "I have an idea. What if we put him on my boat? Maybe that'll keep him quiet."

"Snugs? On a kayak? Are you nuts? He's scared of his own shadow. What makes you think he'd want to go kayaking?"

"Well, it's either that or take him home and lock him in the house," said Derek—ever the pragmatic son. Right. And ruin our kayaking adventure? No way.

I sent the kids off in one boat and started talking to the dog—explaining to him why it would be in his best interests to get on my kayak, sit quietly and enjoy the ride. He listened. He got on. He sat down and, after a minute or two, he lay down with his head on his paws and started soaking up the view. I dragged the boat through the waves and hopped on. We cruised out to the edge of the bay. Tourists visiting La Bufadora to see the Blow Hole started pointing at us. Someone sounded an air horn. Someone else blew a conch shell. The kids and I waved. Snugs sat up and struck his most handsome pose. Everyone onshore was impressed. He was finally famous for something besides being a wimp!

Yes, he kayaked with me and the kids right up until the time he died, almost six years later. I wouldn't have dared consider leaving him onshore. The minute one of our boats hit the surf, he was in it, lying down with his head on his paws. I often wondered, though, if he really enjoyed it as much as he acted like he did—or if he was just terribly grateful for not being left behind on the beach.

Snugs was also famous for his magical swimming ability. Whenever I'd swim to the boats and back—whether I was alone or with Sue, Nina or Kit, he'd tag along. He'd also play on the rocks with Derek, and dive in after him. They'd swim together to shore.

Once, in the middle of the night, Ardell woke up. Someone or something had just jumped into bed with her and Jack. She reached down. Soft. Furry. Warm. She flipped on the light. It was Snugs....

Pedro and Amy at the Hat Party

Hat Parties, Chili Cook-offs and Friday Night at Gordos

For the past 22 years, the Gonzalez family from Tijuana has arrived in La Bufadora every Friday around noon, unlocked their doors, set up the kitchen and bar and put the chairs and tables out on the patio. Chuy flips the *Cerrado*—Closed—sign over to *Abierto*— Open, and Gordos is open for business ... until about noon on Sunday. Friday Night at Gordos is the pinnacle of La Buf's social life. Everyone who's in the mood to hang out shows up. The food is great and cheap. The bar is crowded and everyone is laughing.

The weekends-only tradition started about 24 years ago, when Chuy's father, Abel and mother, Estela opened the first Gordos across the street. After two years, it burned down. They stayed home in Tijuana on weekends for a year or so, until Abel started to get bored. "Let's go talk to Toscano and see if we can buy that place across the street," he said to his family. They did the deal and reopened Gordos at its current location in 1980.

The highlight of the year is the annual Hat Party at Gordos. The first Hat Party happened, quite by accident, in 1987. This was before my time, so what follows here isn't my story. This one is courtesy of Vee Webber, a writer and longtime La Bufadora resident. She'll take it from here:

* * * *

"The April night is brisk, cloudless and pulsating with the rhythms of a local *norteño* band. The staccato buzz of the whisk on the snare drum provides the beat as a group inside Gordos howls at the rising full moon. A man stands in the dirt parking lot, smoking a stogie, dressed in a toga with a wreath of bougainvillea on his head.

"'Man,' he comments. 'Nobody told me about the Hat Party. All I had were the flowers and this bed sheet.'

"'It works,' says his friend, Alex, whose large sombrero drips with cooked spaghetti and sauce. His t-shirt claims that he's a '#1 Italian Lover.'"

"As I enter the brick and stucco building, I notice that Alejandra is having a hard time balancing plates. She's wearing a two-foot tall Statue of Liberty crown that someone made her from construction paper, agave spears and tape. The local *policía*—cop—is behind the bar helping with the overwhelming amount of patrons clamoring for Margaritas. As he whirls the blender, the spaceship on top of his NASA baseball cap keeps pace in orbit around his head. Abel is looking dapper in his felt top hat, as Estela adjusts the wedding veil that keeps slipping to one side of her head. Since this is the year of their fiftieth wedding anniversary, their hats are the only ones that seem appropriate.

"This is the Hat Party—usually held on the last Saturday in March or the first Saturday in April—whichever comes closest to April 1st—that marks Abel's birthday.

"The Hat Party came into being when three gringa expatriates, Cindy, Linda and Sylvia, showed up at Gordos with their friend Judy on a Friday night. These women, affectionately known around the ranch as "*Las Loquitas*"—the Crazy Ladies—arrived with a collection of crazy hats for the staff and patrons to wear in honor of April Fool's Day. As they entered Gordos with arms full of decorations, Estela pulled them aside and told them how wonderful it was that they were making a party for Abel's birthday. Las Loquitas ducked out and quickly headed up to their trailer, where they fashioned a special birthday hat for Abel from an old Padres cap and some battery-operated

Christmas lights. Thus, the first Hat Party was born.

"Las Loquitas made note of the date, and when April first came around the following year, they showed up with more hats and birthday decorations. Word got out around Punta Banda that there was a party happening, and the locals came up with other hat designs of their own. Since then, the Hat Party has taken on a life of its own, becoming an all day event with hat making parties at various homes in the area. Music and a buffet were later added at the restaurant, soon followed by commemorative t-shirts.

"When Abel passed away a few years ago, there was much discussion as to whether the Hat Party should continue. But Abel was a man who always loved a party, so the Memorial Hat Party continues to this day. And Abel, you were right when you said 'Ahhh—this is the life!'"

* * * *

I agree. It is "the life." When you walk into Gordos after sunset on the evening of the party, there is a table by the door, piled high with hats. All evening long people play "grab and switch" with them. If someone down the bar has on a hat you covet, or would at least like to try on, all you have to do is walk up to them, pull the hat off their head and switch. Works for me.

* * * *

In about 1994, Pam and Carol, two full-time La Buf residents, came up with the idea of having an annual chili cook-off at Gordos. It's not a serious, official cook-off like the Hussongs Chili Cook-off in the fall. It's a hoot. It usually takes place in the summer, and it's not publicized, but everyone nearby knows about it months in advance.

A huge Tecate beer tent pops up in the parking lot the morning of the event. People start arriving at nine or ten to set up their booths. The signs go up, advertising: "Survivor Chili," "Pedos de Fuego Chili," "Apache Chili," "Shit Hole Hollow Chili," "Bean-o Chili," "Oh Chit Chili." At noon the cooking begins, according to prescribed rules. There are prizes for the best chili and salsa, a raffle, plenty of beer and good eats. Chuy opens up the window from the bar into the parking lot and sells beer from there.

The first and only time I cooked chili was the second year. In my cookbook, I have a recipe called "Casa Salsipuedes Fifteen Bean Chili." *Salsipuedes* means, "Get out if you can." That's what Nina and I named our house, because it was—like the Hotel California—much harder to leave than to arrive. This used to be a favorite recipe of mine. I didn't know, however, that chili cook-off judges frown on the use of beans in chili. I also didn't remember to soak those 15 different kinds of beans overnight. When I woke up in the morning, I panicked. I stuck them in water and prayed. As they cooked over my camp stove in Gordos parking lot that day, I kept on praying. The beans never softened. When anyone came by to take a bite, I cringed, knowing the crunchy beans were not only unpleasant to chew, but that their flavor was bitter too.

After the judging was done, Derek sneaked inside the restaurant to see what place I'd received. He came back laughing. "You got last place, Mom," he said. I never entered the chili cook-off again. I don't think I ever made that recipe again either.

Carson's Tree House

Carson Stories
What Do You Mean, He Lived in a Tree?!

Richard Carson, fondly known as just "Carson," is one of La Buf's local characters. He always wears black sweat pants and sweatshirt or t-shirt, has a long, scraggly beard, a rattail and gray hair. He has a few teeth missing. He's driven any number of dune buggies, always with a rack and compartment on top so he has an unobtrusive place to sleep—away from scorpions—when in transit or between homes. These days he lives in part of Gene's old shop, under Pam's house. His room is cordoned off with blue tarps, as is his bathroom. He has an easy chair, music, a microwave, a refrigerator with icemaker, and he sleeps on the floor under a round plastic patio table. Before that, he lived in a teepee that still stands just outside the door.

"How'd you move up to this place from the teepee?" I asked him not long ago.

"Well, the last time I went to Arkansas, after Linda left me for the fifth time, I sold all my stuff. When I came back, I rented a trailer from Jack and Kay in Campo 8. Then I lived in that camper shell

behind Gordos. I'd unlock and set up the bar on Fridays and break it
all down for them on Sundays. That way I didn't have to pay rent.
When Gene got sick, Pam asked me to come here and take care of the
dogs and the house when they were in the States for his treatments.
After he died, she asked me to stay on because she didn't want to be
alone in the big house. It works. I help out, and I don't have to pay
rent. I don't like to pay rent."

A former Olympic contender who was raised on the beach and
has been an avid surfer and diver forever, Carson has obviously always
marched to the beat of his own drummer. He's been married to his second wife for 41 years, even though they haven't lived together in eons.
She came to his 70th birthday party at Gordos, though, with their son,
Brian. Everyone dressed like Carson that night, with blackened teeth,
black sweat pants, head bands and any other Arkansas accouterments
they could come up with.

Carson first came to live in Baja around 1980, settling into a
place called Laguna Percebú about 20 miles south of San Felipe. He
had a dune buggy with a rowboat on top. For the first few months, he,
his dog and his American girlfriend, the "Dragon Lady," slept in the
rowboat under a blue tarp while he built his tree house.

"By the way," he told me. "All four of my last girlfriends have
been 4'11" tall with long blonde hair and '38s.' Let's see. There was the
Dragon Lady, then 'Mona Seashells'—a prostitute out of Vegas who
looked like a blonde Mona Lisa. Then there was the 'Frog Lady,' then
Linda. They only lasted about a year—except Linda. She lasted over
ten.

"The Dragon Lady and I slept in the tree house because it was
way too hot to sleep in a trailer. To get by, we sold bundles of *palo de
arco*, or ironwood for two bucks apiece. It got up to about 125 degrees
there in the summer. I'd take a block of ice and a six pack and bury it
in the sand. If I didn't, it would melt within an hour. About a year into
this adventure, I went up to the States to check on my retirement.
When I came back, my girlfriend was gone. So was the dog."

He left for the Pacific coast shortly thereafter, where he's
mostly been ever since. He lived in San Miguel, on the north side of
Ensenada, surfing every day, with the Frog Lady, the next in the lineup
of 4'11" girlfriends. He surfed every day until his retirement was cut
and he had to move back to Huntington Beach. There he lived in a
borrowed trailer and dove for Pismo clams. He also collected alu-

minum cans in a container on the back of a bicycle, ran them over with his dune buggy, loaded them into his boat and delivered them to the recycling facility by water.

"I got a dollar apiece for those clams. I did even better collecting cans. In two weeks, I made 98 bucks."

When he first came to Punta Banda to live, in the mid-'80s, Rancho Packard was just a piece of bare land. There were no facilities, and no one there, except over Fourth of July when hundreds of people showed up. He brought Linda there later on, and built a shack. He began carving and painting faces on coconuts, and then doing Picasso-like paintings of the coconut faces. Still, he dove, he surfed, he kayaked, he fished.

These days he mostly just hangs out. "I got real bored about a year ago and went up to Manny, you know ... Celia's Manny." I nodded. "He drives one of those big 18-wheelers. I asked him if I could come along one time. For $15 we got insurance so I was legal, then we hit 18 states in 18 days and drove 7,000 miles. We had real comfortable double bunk beds in that truck. I read paperback westerns to him all the way. We took secondary roads through the mountains of West Virginia; we crossed the Continental Divide with 15 feet of snow. We stopped at a truck stop in Reno where we had our own trucker's casino. I went into the Wal-Mart in Denver where my daughter works. I hadn't seen her in 10 years. I had her paged. Totally surprised her. I had a great time, but I was wore out by the time I got home. Don't think I could do that again."

"What about that time you and Lee took that sailboat trip down here from somewhere up north? You know, the trip from hell?" I asked.

He laughed. "That guy was one mean son of a bitch … a real asshole. He owed, like $2,600 in slip rental for that boat up in Oxnard. We had to sneak out at night so he didn't have to pay the money. It was supposed to take us four days to get here. It took eight. We had no radio and the Honda backup motor didn't work. It was a 26-foot sailboat and it barely moved some days. By the time we got into the bay here, I was ready to drown the guy. Everyone was sure we were lost at sea anyway. Boy, did Linda ever cuss him out! Then he up and died three months later. Go figure...."

Ann and Terry

Three Strikes and You're On!
How I Met Terry—May through July 1998

When I met Terry, I'd been on a sabbatical from relationships for the better part of a year and a half. I was tired of getting them wrong—and decided to take a break and try to figure some things out.

I wasn't "there yet" on Memorial Day weekend of 1998. I went down with my kids, my friend Jacqueline and her two kids, who were the same ages as mine. We left after school on Friday, and got to Nina and John's house about sunset. (It wasn't half mine anymore, as I'd sold out to her ... but I could still stay there.) The girls staked out the living room couches. The boys pitched a tent on the slab below the deck. We made sure they left room for a couple of our guy friends, who were due Saturday, to pitch a second tent. Jacqueline and I were stylin'—we got the bedrooms.

We got everyone situated, fed and left them playing Scrabble by candlelight around ten. I didn't want to miss Friday Night at Gordos, but I feared, as we drove down the dark dirt roads, that we were too late.

"Lights still on?" I asked her.

"Yep." We parked in front. The Cerrado sign greeted us. We went inside anyway, because we could see a few bodies through the window.

"Not open," called Chuy from behind the bar.

"No?"

"No. Come back mañana."

"Okay."

We got back in the car and headed home, disappointed. " Wait. How'd we miss this?" I asked, pulling over to the side of the road just below Gordos patio. "Lights and cars at Lyn's house. Let's see what's up."

We knocked on the door and looked inside. It looked like the whole of Gordos bar had emptied out and relocated to the next closest venue. There had to be at least 20 people in Lyn's tiny house. The music was blaring. The scene was full tilt boogie.

Lyn motioned us in from behind her bar. We came inside, greeted people I already knew and met several new ones. I was talking to a lady with flaming red hair when someone tapped me on the shoulder. I turned. It was a nice-looking guy about six feet tall with rose-colored glasses, salt and pepper hair and gentle brown eyes. He introduced himself and handed me a beer.

We talked a little that night, but the revelry didn't last long. Jacqueline and I left shortly thereafter. I forgot about the guy.

Fast-forward a month or so to Fourth of July weekend. I'd been hanging out at the beach, kayaking with Steve, Tim, Tim, Pat, Lanae, Kenny, Darrell, Judy and a bunch of other firemen and their women from Orange County. There are a lot of firemen in Baja, and La Bufadora is no exception. I've always wondered a few things about firemen. Why is it that they are uniformly good-looking, well built and really cool? Are these attributes listed as requirements in their job descriptions? It would appear so. Anyway, I've always been game for hanging out with guys that fit that bill. Steve had lured me into the El Dorado on that late summer afternoon on the pretenses of wanting to buy me one of their "Ham-stirred Margaritas." Yeah, he was slurring a bit, but I knew what he meant and I knew that the El Dorado, known in La Buf as "Fred's" (after the owner) had the best Margaritas around. Pure and simple. Tequila, Controy and lime. On the rocks. No salt for me. Not one to pass up a free drink, I drove up, parked, went inside and grabbed a barstool.

Across the bar from me, a familiar-looking guy waved. All the firemen knew him, but I couldn't place him. He came over, re-introduced himself and reminded me that I had met him at Lyn's a month or so previously. We chatted a bit, and that was that. I left soon after and forgot about him. Again.

Three weeks later, my head was in a different place. All of a sudden, I was in the mood to meet a man. I was in La Bufadora again. It was Friday Night at Gordos and this time, I wasn't too late. I came in, said my hellos and sat down at the bar. I felt a tap on my shoulder. It was that good-looking, six-foot tall guy with the salt and pepper hair and rose-colored glasses. He had two Sol cervezas and passed one to me. "Hi Ann," he said.

Uh oh. There was no way I could remember his name. So I said, "Hi. Thanks." I swallowed. "I hate to admit this, but I forgot your name."

He smiled. "Terry," he said.

"No wonder," I said to myself. "Terry. Rhymes with Jerry—my recent ex." No wonder I didn't remember.

We talked that night for hours. I was down for a week, so we saw each other several times. By his fifty-first birthday, the following Friday, when I had to leave, we were smitten with each other ... and we've been together ever since.

However ... to get the full impact of this story, you have to hear Terry's side. He was with his buddies Ron and Mark that first night in May at Lyn's house. He and Ron (both retired firemen, by the way) noticed me when I walked in. Ron nudged Terry. "Did you see that?" he said. Terry didn't say anything, because he was already on his way over to where I was standing.

"I have to meet this lady," were the words running through his head.

After that, he claims he semi-stalked me all over Punta Banda. He was spending the whole summer there, so every weekend he'd ride his motorcycle into La Buf and look for me. It was a little disheartening when I kept forgetting who he was ... but he persevered, and I'm grateful. After all ... boys 'n beers in Baja rule. Doesn't matter if you're 16 or 46....

Sunset from Nina's house

The Romantic Airplane Vacation That Almost Was
August 1999

For the first decade that I was a single mom, I never went on a "romantic vacation." For me, those two words immediately conjure up images of airplanes, passports ... palapas, aquamarine seas, sandy beaches, 360 degree sunsets and warm, balmy climes and drinks with umbrellas in them. English is not spoken. If it is, it's with an accent. The kids are at home, of course and there's no washing machine, computer, telephone or carpool duty to perform. Now, it's fairly obvious that I haven't been deprived of foreign travel—not in Mexico. Nor, during that decade, was I deprived of weekends away from my kids. It's the one thing my married friends used to begrudge me—those every other weekend breaks I got from parenting. Of course, they could whine all they wanted. They'd been on plenty of airplane vacations with their spouses over the years ... something I longed to do.

I had the frequent flyer miles stored up on my Visa card when the invitation came that summer. My Cabo amigos, John and Mary Bragg, were planning a major bash for John's 65th birthday. It was to be at their second home in Ajijic, near Lake Chapala, a mountainside resort just outside Guadalajara. About 30 of their friends were coming, including Terry and me. We cashed in our miles and got free tickets. We booked a hotel right on the lake. We got our passports in order, and drooled while we fantasized about the trip.

We'd be visiting the Herradura tequila factory, watching a ballet folklórico, dining at an exquisite restaurant in a 300-year-old colonial hacienda in Guadalajara. Other outings included a trip to Tlaquepaque, noted for its Indian folk art, and a rancho where we'd dance to Mexican music under the stars. There was even going to be a "Roast" for John and I was asked to participate.

I got some photos converted into slides and practiced my speech. Mary, the consummate planner (one of her Cabo businesses is Weddings in Paradise), had allotted plenty of time for wandering about on our own and soaking up the scenery and culture. Lake Chapala is 5,000 feet above sea level—up in the semi-tropical mountains just east of Puerto Vallarta. In August we could expect temperatures in the 80s during the day, with perfect, cool evenings. Ooh la la....

The kids were off to their dad's. I had all my clothes laid out and I was already half-packed. Then, two days before we were scheduled to leave, Terry's oldest brother passed away. Next morning he was on his way to Maui for the funeral and I was turning in my frequent flyer miles. I wasn't a big enough person to go on a romantic airplane vacation alone—I just wasn't. Nina offered me the use of the Boof house. So, on my scheduled departure date, instead of flying in a jet to an exotic locale, I was flying down the highway in my blue Vanagon, with Snugs for company—headed, once again—to La Bufadora.

Once I got over feeling sorry for myself, I actually enjoyed the time alone in the house on the hill. I hung out with my neighbor Amy a lot. In fact, it was the first time we spent a substantial amount of time together alone ... and we found that we hung out well together. We kayaked and read magazines together at the Boof Beach Club. We cooked dinner together. We went to Friday Night at Gordos. The next day was chili cook-off. Amy entered. I, not having expected to be there, had the perfect excuse not to. Instead, I made the rounds, tasting, chatting and sipping cerveza.

By Sunday, Amy and I were stationed on my deck, taking turns with the binoculars as we checked out every white Ford pickup truck cruising down the hill into town. (Do you have any idea how many white pickups there are in the world?) On Monday morning I spotted it. Or rather, Amy did. She had the binoculars at that moment.

"Does it have red letters that say 'FORD' on the tailgate?" I asked her. It sure did.

"Does it have an egg-shaped decal on the back window?"

"Yup," she said.

"Is it a four-by-four?"

"It's him, Ann."

It was Terry. In person, and with a major case of jet lag. He'd gotten in after midnight the night before and headed out at dawn.

We only got to spend two nights together that week, but we were together. It was warm. The sunsets were great, the computers and phones were stateside, and we even slept in.

I had to wait another year and a half for that romantic airplane vacation. It was to the Riviera Maya, and it was worth the wait. But, I'm a gypsy at heart. Hitting the road or taking off in a plane is my favorite thing on earth. I love the idea of heading off into the unknown. New people. New places. New scenery. New music, food, culture. Adventure. I crave it all like a drug. And I'm certain that one day I will visit John and Mary at Ajijic and spend time in Guadalajara and Lake Chapala ... with Terry.

It's a dog's life....

Gonzo, the Baja Beach Dog, Relays the Story of How He Got to Cardiff Christmas Vacation 1999

"Hey. What's up with this cat, anyway? Every time I come near her, she either runs away or growls and hisses at me. C'mon Elsa, all I want to do is play. You ditz....

"Oh. Hi. I guess I should introduce myself. The name's Gonzo. Used to be Taco back when I lived at the surfer camp on Playa San Pedrito way, way far away in Todos Santos, Baja California Sur. In those days I was one carefree pup, let me tell you. I got up every morning just as the sky was starting to get pink. I stretched, rolled in the sand, shook and took off in search of playmates. Being a surf beach, there were always plenty of dogs around, so I didn't lack for entertainment. After goofing around a while, I got bored and wandered off to do my business. Next it was time to rummage through trash cans sniffing out leftover people food. After breakfast, it was on to the restrooms to drink out of the leaky faucet where the surfer dudes and dudettes brushed their teeth and washed their faces.

"Ah, the life! The rest of the day I ran on the beach, chased birds, romped with other dogs and napped in the shade under a car, van or camper. Every once in a while, some kindly human would make a big fuss over me. 'What a cute, cute puppy,' they'd say. Whenever I heard those words, you can bet I knew I was in luck. Big time. Food! Dog biscuits! Fresh water! Lots of loving! Even a totally cool hemp collar handmade for me by a chick from Colorado!

"I guess you've probably figured out by now why I speak such good English, being a Mexican mutt and all. Well, of course it's because I was born on a really big beach with killer waves. Surfers came to camp there from all over—even as far away as Alaska and Japan. I loved my life there, except for the time that the wasted guy spilled hot candle wax on me. That hurt! So did the kick in the ribs I got from that other jerk in the Range Rover when I peed on his ice chest. You better believe I was a little more careful about whom I hung out with after that.

"So anyway, now you know where I came from and you're probably wondering what I'm doing writing to you from Los Estados Unidos. Well, it all started on Christmas Eve. A nice, big motor home (think shade) pulled into the campground. Usually those big rigs parked over in the RV Park, where I wasn't welcome—but not this one. These guys apparently wanted to experience the surfer lifestyle up close and personal. That'd be my guess. Anyway, there was a man, a woman and a dog. An old yellow dog who didn't move around much. Didn't eat much either and didn't mind sharing his food with me. All right! Merry Christmas to me! I decided to hang close and check things out.

"The man took to me right away. In fact, before the sun went down he'd given me a new name. Gonzo. Hmm, not bad. Much better than Taco. It always made me a little nervous being named after something humans ate, if you know what I mean. The thought of ending up on somebody's combo platter didn't excite me in the least. No way, José. Absolutely not. The lady gave me dog biscuits. Yum! The next morning, on Christmas, she gave me eggs. Without any sand on 'em. Wowsers!

"They stayed around a couple days more and introduced me to some of their new friends. One guy named Lee, from Oregon, really took to me. I kept hearing him say to Ann and Terry (the motor home people) that he wanted to find a Baja beach dog to adopt. When I heard that, I was a little confused. Adopt? What did that mean? Everyone I ever got close to in Todos Santos left eventually. Did 'adopt' mean they didn't leave? I was hoping so. I started hanging really close to Lee.

"Then the motor home people left. But Lee didn't, thank God. I moved in with him and his group up on the bluff by the big palapa. Never had I eaten better food or gotten more love. It was the life, man! Then the motor home people came back. With a boy and a girl, no less—who had apparently flown (like the birds?) into La Paz (wherever that is) after visiting their dad for Christmas. I heard Lee tell the four of them that he couldn't adopt me after all, but that I'd be perfect for them. Perfect. Now that had a nice ring to it! Ann, Terry and the kids had a family conference, which I eavesdropped on, of course.

"Oh my God! They decided to adopt me and take me to a vet (think ouch) in Loreto on their way home. So, next morning, the boy, Derek chased me down after my morning routine and led me to the motor home. I'd eaten so much good food that I threw up on Gayle's lap about an hour or so out of Todos Santos. I thought for sure they were gonna eject me from the vehicle at that point, or at least whack me. But they didn't. They just oohed and aahed and 'Poor Gonzoed' me. Then they cleaned it up and sent me to sit up front on Ann's lap where I could get more fresh air. Now that was the life, let me tell you!

"Five days later we landed in La Bufadora. Now, this was my favorite stop. I could run free there. I met a lovely young dog named Pearl and immediately deflowered her. I went to the beach and chased waves and birds to my heart's content. It was colder there than Todos Santos, but I loved it. My new humans stayed in a house there, so I'm guessing I'll get to go back again. I hope so. I much prefer it to my new residence, in Cardiff-by-the-Sea, U.S.A.. But then I shouldn't complain about this place. After all, I have a choice of four couches to sleep on, fresh water on demand in one of two toilet bowls, a cat to chase (weirdo that she is), a boxer to play with next door, a harness, a leash (yuck!), a name tag and all kinds of majorly cool stuffed toys to disembowel. Next week I even get to go get fixed—whatever that means...."

Ann and Terry hanging out on the patio with Gonzo

How We Found Our Baja Dream House
Spring 2000

Part One:
STUMBLING UPON A STAIRWAY TO HEAVEN....

Almost immediately after I sold my interest in the La Buf house to Nina, I regretted it. I went into instant withdrawals. The summer of 1999 we semi-camped at Terry's place on the other side of Punta Banda—at Agua Caliente—about 20 minutes from La Buf. His bachelor pad is a tiny, dark and dingy place, all done up in shades of brown and beige. It's just down the road from (and highly reminiscent of) the site of my dad's old fishing shack. Like Dad's, Terry's is most definitely not chick friendly. There's one main room—a kitchen-living room combo. There's also a bathroom with a tiny shower and a toilet that's a crusty brown on the inside. I tried and tried, but made no headway whatsoever in scrubbing it clean! There's no bedroom, but there is a patio. A dirt road on one side and a tall block wall on the other, border, as Terry calls it, the cabaña. The wall blocks out the sight of the wall-to-wall campers that converge there every summer, but it fails to block out the noise. The people who camp there love ATVs. They love jet skis. They love to party and they love fireworks. They shoot them off at all hours of the day and night, all summer long. This cabaña has no view, but it's only a minute walk to the beach.

When I first met Terry, he lived there with two dogs, Oso Negro and Brava. They were big dogs, I might add—a lab mix and a Rottweiler—who slept with him on one of the two couches that doubled as beds. He called it the "Dog House." No misnomer there. In the summer of 1999, we had just bought a motor home, thinking that would compensate for the missing La Buf house. We could travel more, right? And we could park the RV next to the Dog House and use it as a master bedroom, so we'd not only have a place to sleep, but a little privacy too. I tried really, really hard to overlook the brown, to see past the cramped, dark space and to ignore the campground noises from next door. I ordered myself to focus instead on the long beach with its warm water, gentle waves.

I knew by August that I could no longer pull this off. I hadn't even made it through one summer. "Let's get real, here, Ann," I told myself. "You've been boofed. You're spoiled. Rotten." I missed the postcard views from the hillside out over the water. I missed the peace and quiet. I missed watching the pelicans at sunset as they cruised around the bay. I missed the seals, the dolphins, and the whales. I missed being within walking distance from my friends. Seller's remorse? You bet. I had it and I had it bad. I might mention also that I wasn't terribly quiet or gracious about it either.

Fast-forward to March, 2000. Terry and I had decided we would find a house. All over La Bufadora are abandoned houses. We'd been exploring them for months. The day before we headed south for Saint Patrick's Day, I told Terry we had to go to the office and ask Miguel Toscano if he would show us what was available. Maybe, just maybe, we'd missed something as we'd scoured the ranch trying to find our dream home, or some facsimile thereof. We'd just applied for a second mortgage on the house in Cardiff. We had some money coming in and we were ready to spend it. The night before we left, I dreamed of a house on a cliff overlooking the ocean. In the disjointed way of dreams, it was and was not familiar terrain to me, but I knew the house was somewhere near Jerry's. I told Terry about the dream. He shrugged his shoulders and said, "Who knows? We'll just have to see what Miguel has to show us."

We got to the office about 2:00 p.m. and found Miguel. "I have only one house on the water to show you," he said. I'd been adamant about being on the water. Hey. If you're going to find your dream home, I figured, you might as well go for what you really, really want. And after doing time in the Dog House, I knew I really, really wanted to be in the front row, with no one between me and the ocean ... if that was anywhere in the realm of possibility.

He showed us the house we call the "Road House." It sort of hangs on the edge of the cliff, right to the side of the road, looking like it might slip into the ocean at any moment. There is a trailer in back that houses the kitchen and bathroom and a couple of funky rooms in front. It gave me vertigo. There just had to be something better, didn't there?

I asked Miguel that question. He scratched his head and nodded, slowly. "Well, there is this green house. We might be able to sell that one." He pointed up the hill and to the right. It was a faded shade of lime green with a zigzag asbestos roof that looked like white rickrack. It was kitty-corner to Jerry's house (just like in my dream) and terraced up the hill in three levels. I'd snooped in about every abandoned house in La Bufadora. I'd even lived practically next door for a while. But I had never walked up that long stairway to see what the house was all about. I'd figured that it was situated in a way that it couldn't possibly have a view—even if it was on the edge of the bay. Wrong.

We walked up the 38 stairs. At the top, my breath caught in my throat. There was a huge concrete patio with a gnarly old myroporum tree in the center. A stonewall with natural plants separated the patio from the cliffs below—solid granite cliffs that went down 85 feet to tide pools and turquoise sea below. The water stretched out endlessly in front of me. I looked across the bay and saw the Blow Hole shoot up its waterspout. I turned. I looked inside. There were three big sliders in the front room. I opened one and stepped in. The house was gray, unfinished block and plaster with concrete floors. Aside from lots of trash and some ugly graffiti on the walls, there were three barbecues, some patio furniture, several roll away beds and a crusty old kitchen unit that wasn't hooked up to anything. Other than that, it was empty. "Terry," I called. "Come in here and see. This house is a blank canvas!"

He didn't even turn around. "Who cares what it looks like

inside?" he called back at me. "Come look at the view!"

"Can we buy this house?" we asked Miguel.

"Maybe. Soon. I will talk to my father."

Uh oh. I didn't want someone else swooping in here and snagging this place. No way. I decided to push my luck. "Well, would it be okay if we bring our motor home and camp in the driveway? We'll just use the patio?"

He smiled. "Sure. No problem."

We spent the afternoon on the patio, and waited until after sunset to head back to the Dog House. We had a cooler of beer and some snacks, so we were set. What we didn't have was a bathroom. As I was looking around for a secluded place to relieve myself, Terry said,

"Hey. You gotta pee on the tree."

"Why?"

"Because you'll put your mark on the place, just like Snugs or Gonzo do. It'll guarantee that we get this house."

"Well, then you have to do it too," I told him.

We did.

Part Two:
SQUATTING IN AN ABANDONED HOUSE
WITH FOUR TEENAGERS

The week before Easter, called *Semana Santa* in Mexico, Terry and I took four teenagers to the house we were so desperately coveting. We'd checked with Miguel again to see if we could buy the house, but he still had no answer. The elderly Señor Toscano hadn't been well of late. We knew that sooner or later he'd be back on the ranch again, and when he showed up, we wanted it to be clear that we were first in line to buy this house. We wanted to stake our claim, and what better way to do it than by squatting, right?

So there we were, off to camp out for a week in a house with no running water or electricity. Whoever built this house, did an amazing job—they just walked away before they finished it. The year 1974 is scratched into the concrete on top of the patio wall, so we knew they'd started working on the house nearly 30 years ago. Aside from its million-dollar view, the house is solid, constructed of block and rock with a watertight roof, windows with screens and blinds and one and a half bathrooms. What it lacked was a functioning kitchen, water supply and electricity. Well, there wasn't any paint on the walls (except the graffiti) and the floors were concrete, but those things didn't deter me. On the contrary. My mom was an interior designer and I inherited her love of decorating. This was going to be a challenge I would relish ... if we ever got to buy the house, that is.

We brought our motor home down with us that week. We also brought a camping table and stove, tons of cleaning supplies and permission from the next-door neighbor to run a hose from his house into the kitchen and bathrooms.

Terry and I had told the kids that the house was full of trash and dead critters. But, hey, we'd also told them they were gonna love it—after the work was done! Believe me, I'm not opposed to child labor, and six people can clean a place up a whole lot faster than two. We were ready, set, go for an adventure—all six of us. We pulled up on Monday and started taking loads of stuff up the stairs. The first things we brought were brooms, rags and black plastic trash bags. It took two hours to clean the place up. Terry's job was the worst. Only one bathroom door was open at that point, and the toilet in there was way, way gross. He took it off, hauled it outside, turned it upside down and turned on Frithjof's hose full-blast. Voila!

Derek's buddy, Andrew, pried the second bathroom open. The boys screamed bloody murder when they got inside. This toilet was okay, but the pink porcelain tub was full of dirt, dead mice and roaches. They tried to disappear, but I made 'em get the dead stuff out and then the girls cleaned. By sunset, we had one fully functioning bathroom (if you consider turning on the hose to fill the toilet tank when you want to flush it and bathing with a hose in cold water fully functional) and another toilet that could be used if flushed with a bucket of water. Terry attached a second hose to the first with a Y-valve and ran that hose through the kitchen window. We now had running water. We put empty, beat-up Styrofoam coolers that we'd found in the lower room under the sink, so we could do dishes. We unloaded the camping stove onto the folding table. Between that and those three barbecues, we were good to go! We had two big ice chests full of food, a boom box, propane lanterns and lots of candles. We inventoried the furniture in the house: a table and chairs, plenty of patio furniture, a coffee table and five rollaway beds. Gayle and Kristen set up camp in the living room. Derek and Andrew took over one of the two bedrooms. Our master suite was still the motor home.

On day two we tackled the patio. Terry and I pruned the half-dead myroporum tree to give it a bonsai look. Derek and Andrew climbed the neighbor's eucalyptus trees, sawed off the dead branches and hauled them over to the nearby fire pit. We were knee-deep in trimmings when Bucky and Russ rounded the corner with a cooler of beer in hand. Russ handed us a little decal that said, "Squatters" on it. We dropped our pruning shears, popped open beers and took a serious Pacifico break.

In my mind, there's no better beer on earth in my mind than an ice cold Pacifico—especially in Mexico. After a lot of hard work, the beer always tastes even better than usual. The kids took off—free at last. The boys headed down to the tide pools and the girls to the beach to work on their sunburns. The boys kayaked, jumped off rocks into the freezing cold ocean and swam to shore. The girls shopped at the Mall and went hiking. Gayle whipped the other three in round after round of dominoes, using the jail house rules Derek had learned the previous summer from Terry's brother, Homey, at the Dog House. She reigned all week as the domino queen. Their conversations during these games were bizarre, although I did my best not to eavesdrop. Every time Terry or I would wander indoors, all we'd hear was a chorus of "How 'bout them Padres?" followed by raucous laughter.

Oh, one last thing. I forgot to ask our neighbor, Frithjof which *pila*—water tank—was his. I asked around and no one on the ranch knew—not even Tony Sanchez—the waterman. So we guessed, and we guessed wrong. We paid to fill the wrong pila on Thursday and ran out of water an hour later. From then on we had to forego the cold showers from the hose and flush the toilets with melted cooler water until we figured out which was the right pila. But hey, it was an adventure none of us will ever forget.

Part Three:
WHY DON'T WE DO IT IN THE ROAD?

It finally happened—almost two months to the day after we'd first climbed the stairway to heaven. We'd been squatting at least every other weekend (plus Spring Break) at the house. In those two months, we hadn't been able to talk to Señor Toscano. Each time, before we came down, I'd call Miguel and make sure it was okay to camp there. We were still living out of the motor home for the most part. We had the water hose thing down pretty well, so we were combination squatter-campers.

That day, we pulled up around one o'clock. As we hiked our coolers and other gear up the stairway, we noticed the Toscano's car at the Road House below us. I thought I saw him. The Señor! Wondering what would happen next, I kept schlepping stuff up to the patio. Stopping to soak in the view, I noticed a pod of dolphins frolicking in the bay below me. Good omen, perhaps?

A few minutes later, I was inside unpacking supplies when there was a knock on the door. It was Laia, a lady I'd known for years that worked for Señor Toscano. In her rapid-fire Spanish, which I somehow usually manage to understand most of, she told me that he was very upset that we were there ... that we did not have the right to be in this house ... it was his house ... that we couldn't stay there without paying ... and who did we think we were to just move in, anyway? I explained to her, as best I could, that we had Miguel's permission ... that we were interested in buying the house, but had been waiting to talk to the Señor. She told me I needed to come down and speak to the Señor and immediately explain this to him myself.

I brushed my hair, Terry and I finished our "welcome beers" and then we fairly flew over to the Road House. Señor Toscano met us in the road. I told him what I had just told Laia. My Spanish, which fluctuates on any given day from stumbling and mediocre to adequate, (don't ask me why) was flowing along pretty well that day. Thank God, because neither he nor Laia speak English. He thought a while. Then, in Spanish, he told me that he would be willing to sell us the house. "How much is that?" I asked him.

He smiled at me in his endearing, benevolent way. His eyes twinkled with mischief. "$15,000" he said. "And $200 a month for rent."

Terry and I exchanged looks. We'd discussed (endlessly) how much this house might end up costing us if we were able to buy it. We'd hoped we could get it for about $15,000 ... but we hadn't wanted to get our hopes up.

Fifteen thousand dollars? Sold! At that point my Spanish gave out. I fumbled and bumbled my way through our thanks. We shook hands, right there in the dirt road between our new house and the Road House. We tried to saunter casually over to visit Bucky and Russ, who were working on a house nearby. Finally out of sight of the Señor, we burst through the front door and screamed, "We got it! We got the house! We got the house!"

After a round of hugs, they calmed us down some. "The Señor takes checks," Bucky reminded us. "Grab your checkbook and head on over to the office. Write him a check. Get a receipt. Get started on your land lease." I'd forgotten ... of course he takes checks. An hour later, we emerged from Señor Toscano's office, receipt in hand. We were legal. We had our house. After we signed our contract, the Señor looked at Terry and said, "*Bienvenidos a la familia de Rancho La Bufadora*"—Welcome to the La Bufadora family. They shook hands. I smiled and sneaked a peek at Terry. I could see that his eyes were welling up. So were mine. To this day, he chokes up whenever he tells people about that day....

OBE's new life of leisure

OBE-Juan the Baja Cat Emigrates to California
July 2000

"Meow. Hi! Yes, I'm a cat. Well, a kitten really. Gayle weighed me at the frutería in Cantú a few weeks ago and I only weighed about a kilo. That's 2.2 pounds. At the vet's last week I was up to four pounds! So I guess you could say I'm kind of small—but I'm growing fast! I have a nice fat belly these days. Oh yeah, baby ... a full belly. Not full of beetles and crickets, but full of crunchy, yummy fish-flavored morsels of dried cat food and Fancy Feast. Boy oh boy. Did I ever score or what?

"My name is OBE-Juan, pronounced just like that Jedi dude in Star Wars. But please don't mistake me for him. My official moniker is Old Blue-Eyed Juan. Yes, I am a Mexican. Or I was. Now I'm half Mexican and half gringo. That's cool. Since goofy old Gonzo is too, and he got to tell the story of how Ann and her family adopted him, it's only fair that I get to tell my story too. Right? Okay. Here we go.

"I was born in La Bufadora around Cinco de Mayo, which, by the way is not Mexican Independence Day. For your information, I know my history and May 5th is the date of the Battle of Puebla, where the Mexican Army soundly defeated the French back in 1862. It doesn't even mark the end of French rule however; because the French went on to capture Mexico City a year later. They put their guy, Maximillian, on the throne, where he ruled as emperor 'til 1867, when he was executed. The real Mexican Independence Day is celebrated on September 16. Well, actually, the parties really get going the night before when *El Grito*—The Shout—is read from the Palacio Municipal in Mexico City. If I recall correctly, this happened in 1810 when Father Hidalgo—known as the Father of Mexico—first proclaimed it.

"But anyway, I'm digressing. Where was I? Oh. Yeah. There were three other kittens in my litter. Our mom was mostly Siamese and our dads were any one of several tomcats on the ranch. Mom liked the guys. I was the only one who looked like her, though. We were born in the back room of Celia's Mini Market and lived quite happily in a cardboard box while we were nursing. People would come in from time to time and pick me up, cuddle me, kiss me and make me purr. I loved that!

"But one day, when I was about six weeks old, everything changed. Mom took us outside to play in the sunshine. There were dogs out there! One of them decided to play with one of my sisters. He picked her up by the back of the neck and spun her around like a toy. Mom hissed and scratched at the dog. She even drew blood on its nose, but by the time she convinced it to drop my sister, it was too late. She was dead, her neck broken.

"Mom was shook up, believe me. She kept licking and licking her, trying to bring her back to life. It didn't work. Mom kind of lost it after that. She ran off with a couple of tomcats and we never saw her again. It was awful. My brother disappeared one night when he was out hunting for something to eat. Then it was just the two of us. All we could find to eat was the occasional bug or two. They were crunchy and wiggled a lot too—especially those big beetles that spit and hiss when you flip them upside down, but they tasted pretty okay, actually, and we got pretty darn good at catching them. Water was hard to find and we were thirsty a lot, as it was starting to be summer and the days were heating up. We slept curled up together at night under an abandoned house. In the mornings we'd get up really early to lap the dew off the leaves before the sun came out. It was okay, but we were hungry, thirsty, scared and lonely most of the time.

"People came by from time to time. We wanted so much to

meow at them and ask them to scoop us up their arms and carry us away to somewhere nice and cozy like Celia's back room. But most of them had dogs with them and that freaked us out. So we hid alone under our house. I was out hunting bugs one early evening while my sister was asleep. When I got back, there was a little Mexican girl in front of our hideout. She had my sister in her arms and was singing to her and petting her. I could hear the purring from way, far away. As I hid in a bush, I watched my sister leave my life forever. I was alone now, and so lonely.

"I knew my only hope was to find a human of my own—without a dog. I met a real nice lady named Bucky who fed me a little cat food and petted me one day. But she had this wild and crazy dog named Pearl, so I had to pass on adopting her. Enter Gayle and Derek. I saw them trailing behind their adults a few days later. The adults had a dog, but by this time I was so hungry and lonesome that I didn't care. I meowed my loudest from under my abandoned house. Gayle heard me. She came running over, found me and picked me up. She loved me and put me inside her sweatshirt. She and Derek took me home with them and fed me milk and cheese. They gave me a warm bath. They picked out all my fleas and cleaned my ears. I got to sleep on their beds. By the next day, Derek had built me a fort in the tree on their patio and I was able to sunbathe up there all afternoon out of reach of that goofy dog, Gonzo. He put bowls of food and water up there for me too. I was set.

"I crossed the border on July sixth without incident. Life is heavenly now. I like riding in the car, I like my new houses—both of them. I've even become best buddies with Gonzo! I adore my new humans. They spoil me rotten! I am one very happy gato—with a very round belly these days—let me tell you. And guess what? They have those twitchy, hissing beetles in Cardiff too! I don't eat 'em anymore, but I catch 'em and toss 'em up in the air for Gonzo to play with!"

* * * *

Postscript:

The last anyone saw OBE-Juan was St. Patrick's Day, 2001. He stayed behind when we went to La Bufadora. I came home that Sunday night without Terry or Gonzo. They'd stayed behind to paint (Terry) and run around like a goofball (Gonzo). No OBE. The kids and I looked everywhere ... for days! But the strangest thing happened at 3:08 a.m. that Monday morning right after I got back. He jumped up onto my stomach, made his usual little "merrr-ow" and started to purr—just like he did about that time every night. I sat straight up and reached for him. He wasn't there. I turned on the light. He wasn't there ... at least not physically. But I believe he visited me for one last little bit of a love session, to say, "I love you and goodbye." Little OBE-Juan, you were only 10 months old when you left us, but you were the coolest cat I ever had ... and you will be missed. Always....

Does it get any better than this?
Photo courtesy of Kim Boeck

Sitting on the Edge of the Bay
July 2000—La Bufadora, Baja California

In my lap is a yellow pad; in my hand a purple pen. I sit on a concrete bench with my feet propped on a rock wall, leaning back against a natural rock outcropping. A cup of coffee steams beside me. The surge of the waves below soothes me. A trio of pelicans soars by. One by one they peel off and glide north across the bay. I look up to watch them and the world is all done up in shades of blue: cobalt for the dark, deep sea next to the pale periwinkle of the sky. The shallower waters are sapphire and aquamarine and laced with foamy white.

I sigh, put my pen down and continue watching. OBE-Juan nips at my toes and scurries after a lizard. The Blow Hole spews water skyward. It's going strong this morning. I get up, walk around the corner and look toward the beach. I notice that the tide's about at midpoint and the swell is coming from the south. This is when La Bufadora blasts the highest. Yes. Sitting down again. That one blew right up to the top of the mountain's saddle. Yesterday we saw a pod of dolphins swimming into the bay, fins sliding in and out of the glassy water. We saw three seals peeking out from the kelp at us. We haven't seen any whales since Memorial Day weekend, but we know that come winter, they'll be cruising by regularly. Pelicans and sea gulls are common year-round. We call our house Pelican Flight, or *Vuelo Pelícano* in Spanish, because we're smack in the middle of their aerial highway. Since we're so high up, the birds often do their fly-bys at or near eye level. Our windows are often splashed with white as the birds roll around the edge of the bay. So is the occasional head or two.

Things have changed a lot in the two months we've owned this house. A few weeks ago we broke down and got a cell phone, but it's only for emergencies. Until the other day we had to charge it at a friend's house because we had no electricity. Everything changed a few days ago—the day the power came on. We'd bought a fridge and stove at a *segunda*—second hand store—in Ensenada, so we were ready. Our house marches like a German bunker up the hillside in three layers, ending at the living room and kitchen that open onto an expanse of patio and ocean. The electricity came in three waves too. The first day was the lower level and the last day was the upper. Between days one and three, a long extension cord powered up our fridge.

A friend of mine who's got a decade on me in La Buf is spastic about the electricity. He resents the modern appliances and blaring lights at night. He despises the idea of gringo-style progress overwhelming and destroying the raw, rugged beauty of our special place. I understand. I hate jet skis, with a fervor that matches my friend Bucky's. The last time they roared into our bay, she trooped onto the beach, her hands on her hips and ever so politely asked them to leave. They left. Our clear waters are reserved for sea creatures, kayaks, divers and those of us swimmers who can stand its chill. It's not a safe harbor for jet skis.

Yet, while ambivalent about progress, I'm glad to be able to freeze ice cubes. Such a simple pleasure—ice water. Such a treat to pull a package of chicken breasts from the freezer and know they'll thaw out just in time to be barbecued for dinner. Such a joy to get up in the middle of the night and not have to stagger around in the dark searching for a flashlight. So cool to plug in our big boom box now and not worry if we're going to run out of D batteries. So luxurious to make a blender drink, use an electric coffee pot and contemplate buying a microwave!

We still use the candles, though. The soft flickering shadows against the wall remind me that this is still a primitive place. They remind me to slow down, to inhale deeply of the beauty around me. Then, and only then do I reconnect with the essence of who I am. Then I remember that life lived at a slower pace is essentially a much fuller life.

This has been a perfect vacation. Even Gayle and Derek have quieted. Without phones, computers, dueling stereos, televisions and friends—they've bonded with one another and us. Even they've become infused with the peaceful magic of living here at the edge of the bay.

Chelsea and Bragg hang Derek and Harry's wet boxers in the windows.

Torrid Tales From Teenage Summer Camp
August 2000

Have you ever bitten off more than you can chew? You know, when that last straw breaks the camel's back with a snap, and you find yourself suddenly, shockingly transformed from a model of congeniality and hospitality into a resentful, raving lunatic? Well, this happened to me during the summer of 2000. More than once, actually. The unfortunate turn of events (or perhaps I should say, swivel of my head) only seems to befall me when I have the noblest intentions, and when I give, give and give until my manners, patience and kindness completely run out. Then I blow up, have to calm down, apologize and do some serious regrouping, promising myself I will not do that again. Oh sure. We just spent 19 days in Mexico. Sound idyllic? Well, it was supposed to be. I wanted nothing more than to give Gayle, Derek and their friends a Baja experience that would linger in their memories forever. Problem was, I let myself be talked into inviting way too many teenagers and way too many grown ups. I ended up doing way too much cooking, cleaning and supervising. We ended up running a teenage summer camp and I was the Camp Director. I was on duty 24-7.

At any given moment we had from three to eight teenage "campers" under our roof, sleeping 'til noon, slurping down sodas and eating like they had just been released from a concentration camp. Derek and Harry followed me around all day, whining in unison, "I'm hungry. Feed me!" I'd just bought a microwave, but apparently they couldn't remember how to use one. The ranks kept swelling the longer we were there. By the last Saturday night, I counted 15 people sleeping in and around our house. Terry (called UT or Uncle Terry) and I. Gayle and her friends Jessica and Chelsea. Joey, Derek and Harry. Our next-door neighbor from Cardiff, Bragg came down with his brother Page. They were supposed to be camp counselors, but ended up regressing and recreating themselves as born-again teenagers. Then Page hooked up with Lindsey, who was visiting Amy. Our old next-door neighbor from Solana Beach, Chuck and his dad, Terry (called PT or Papa Terry) were there too. Chuck was 36 years old at the time, but being in Mex Mode, he backslid a bit as well. He "borrowed" a fire ring from one neighbor and got caught. I had to escort him over the next morning to confess. He showered in another neighbor's outdoor shower and ran the pila dry. He redeemed himself, however. The last morning we were there, he chased down a water truck and refilled the pila.

Finally, there were Uncle Terry's good friends, Mark and Cliff. Cliff overdid it big time on Rattlesnake Tequila at Gordos and spent an entire evening with his head hanging over the edge of a cliff ... before he passed out face up in Mark's truck, that is. The two dogs and one cat were relatively well behaved—at least OBE-Juan was. Gonzo's Mexico girlfriend, Pearl and his American girlfriend, Devin (Bragg's dog) fought over him constantly. They were three whirling, growling dervishes, spinning across the patio and through the house....

It wasn't this crazy the whole time. We started out the first weekend with three teenagers: Gayle, Derek and Chelsea—plus a bunch of others who wandered in and out. By Monday, everyone was gone but my three. Manageable—at least it was once I was able to get them out of bed in the morning. Wanting to teach them the value of teamwork and good, honest labor, I told them I'd give them spending money for helping us paint the house. I tried explaining to them that construction jobs always start early in the day—like 7:00 a.m.—especially in the summer when it gets blazing hot toward noon. The very notion of rising before 10:00 was beyond their comprehension, although they somehow managed to get up before 6:30 for school. To quote Chelsea: "We're teenagers. It's in our job description to be nocturnal." That remark pretty much summed up the mindset of "Teenage Summer Camp."

So we got started every day around 11:00. By noon we were all overheated and crabby. Somehow we managed to keep on painting until we ran out of paint. By then the exterior of the house was almost fully painted—minus the trim and edges of course, which was Terry's and my responsibility. Ninety percent of the upstairs rooms got finished too. The first Thursday the kids decided they wanted to take a kayak adventure around the point to Long Beach, or *Bahía Puerto Escondido* as it's officially called. I let them go, provided they packed four bottles of water apiece, plenty of food, sunscreen, shirts, hats, beach towels and a first aid kit. Terry and I were to have a whole day to ourselves, at least from eleven 'til four. Bummer was, we got in a fight the night before and he walked all the way to the Dog House with Gonzo. This took him about four hours, I think. I was so ticked off at him that I didn't drive over and get him 'til nearly sunset the next day. Well, we'd wanted time alone ... we just hadn't expected to spend it separately.

Another day, the kids took off kayaking again. Gayle had a Rambo-ette moment when she led the flotilla of teen campers in between some rocks and misjudged the wave action. A big set came in and Derek and Harry were tossed off their boats. Derek scrambled onto the back of Chelsea's kayak. Harry ditched his boat and climbed up the rocks and onto shore. Gayle single-handedly rescued both escaped boats, but not before one of them (a borrowed boat of course) was beaten against the rocks, damaging it somewhat. Derek and Harry weren't bothered in the slightest by the incident and went to check out the tide pools. Gayle and Chelsea, on the other hand, were basket cases. They came roaring down the dirt road in my VW van (of course—they never walked anywhere), dragged me aside and simultaneously burst into tears.

"I almost killed everybody, Mommy!" wailed my daughter, the

drama queen.

"I need to call my mommy!" Chelsea wailed, not to be topped. "No, you don't," I said, hugging them both at once. "Not until you calm down. Your mom will freak out and that's not fair. You did a dumb thing, you guys, but fortunately none of you got hurt, and hopefully (please!) you all learned some more respect for the ocean from this....."

Ay yay yay.

The chili cook-off happened to fall in the middle of our 19-day adventure. Instead of entering, which I refuse to do, I'd invited Chuck to come down and cook. I'd help chop and stir so I could bask in some of his glory when he won. He did win third prize too, a few years ago. Chuck used to be an Executive Chef at the Chart House, so his cooking credentials are impeccable. He's my "ringer," and I know he'd never forget to soak his beans. Of course, he knows better than to use beans at all.

The day of the cook-off was followed by the night we had 15 people sleeping in and around our house, so suffice to say, things were a bit on the hectic side. I'd planned to enter the salsa contest, but changed my mind. I was too busy cooking breakfast, lunch and dinner, washing dishes, dumping the bucket under the sink, flushing the toilets with a bucket and a hose and making runs into town for more provisions. Chuck had two assistants, however, Terry and Terry, a.k.a. UT and PT. Nina, her friend Paula and I got to judge the salsas. While some people might complain about this, we were in salsa heaven. After all, we are serious salsaholics and we also had sufficient cerveza with which to cool our palates.

Chuck didn't win that year, but our neighbors from Cardiff and La Bufadora, Cathy and John did. Their chili was called "Survivor Chili." In commemoration of the TV show, they decorated their booth with palm trees, hibiscus flowers and a big old plastic rat in a trap. There was a button next to it. Cathy had everyone who came by push that button. The second they did, the rat started jumping and thrashing like crazy, straining against the trap. Everyone asked the same question: "Is there rat meat in your prize-winning chili?" She just laughed.

The next morning I went on strike. All 15 teenagers (this number included the born-again teenagers too) at our house decided that if they wanted to eat, they'd better go out for a $1.50 breakfast. Gayle drove my van down the dirt road to Fred's, which has sadly since closed. On the roof of the van rode Bragg, Chelsea, Joey, Derek and Harry—hooting and hollering. We followed behind in Mark and Terry's trucks—the truck beds loaded with people too. Fred's had been without a breakfast cook for a week or so, and this was the first morning they were back open for business. The place was packed. We carved out a place for ourselves on the patio and proceeded to settle in for what we knew would be a long wait.

After waiting a half hour, Chuck and Papa Terry bailed, deciding to go into Ensenada for fish tacos. Right afterward, one of those characters you see sometimes in a bar in Baja, with a couple of metal cylinders attached to a battery-powered box showed up. He was selling a shock for a buck. Everyone was grossed out, except Bragg, who was in macho-mode and had to try it. He loved it. Page succumbed to sibling rivalry and tried it. Then all the kids got into it. They joined hands in a big circle, with Bragg holding one cylinder and Page holding the other. The guy turned on the juice and they had a group shock. I couldn't look. It was one of those fingernails on the chalkboard moments for me. Major yuck. Oh yeah. Welcome to Teenage Summer Camp.

When I was relating some of our misadventures to the cashier at Trader Joe's the day I got back, Frederick, the guy who was packing my groceries, started laughing out loud. "Man," he said. "You should've charged those kids about $1,000 apiece for their camping experience."

Hey. Maybe that's why I got so burned out. I fed, cleaned up after and entertained that horde for free. Well, the teenagers anyway. Our older guests may have backslid into adolescent behavior for a portion of their vacations, but at least they had their own money and didn't expect me to give them an allowance on Fridays!

Happiness is...

The Boof House Gets a Real Kitchen
Fall 2000

My new Baja kitchen is wonderful, even though the stove isn't hooked up and neither is the hot water because the propane line isn't finished. It's a custom dream kitchen from heaven. The cupboards and counters run in an L-shape around the room. There's a special cupboard that holds the drinking water dispenser. The next cupboard over has shelves for water bottles—called *garrafones*. Underneath it is another cupboard with pullout shelves that were specially designed to hold two empty Pacifico cases. In Mexico, we always save the empty beer bottles and turn them in when we buy more beer. This isn't just a conservation thing; it costs twice as much to buy a box of beer if you don't turn in the empties. There's a handcrafted round Mexican table in the center of the room with four Mexican chairs from Guadalajara. I have more cupboard space here than I do at home, and while I'm cooking, I can turn my head to the right and look out across the patio to the ocean beyond.

    It's finished now, thank God. Finally. Have you ever lived in a house or worked in an office while it was being remodeled? If you have, then you know what a nightmare it can be. I come from a construction family, so I've witnessed something spectacular arising out of chaos and filth many times. I've tiptoed around stacks of plywood and two-by-fours and tried not to trip over piles of block, rocks and sand. I've navigated around power tools, shop-vacs, sawhorses and piles of furniture and boxes covered in plastic to keep the dust out of every imaginable nook and cranny. I lived through an office remodel once and had sinus problems from the dirt for three months. But I still had a place to go home to at night with a functional kitchen and living room. I was still able to take a hot shower whenever I felt like it.

    Remodeling is actually harder than building from scratch. If you're starting from scratch, you get yourself temporary quarters during construction. Not so with remodels. When you're remodeling, you tend to live in and with the insanity. Add to this picture the fact that this house is in Mexico. That makes the whole process a bit more challenging. For one thing, we can't buy everything we need in Mexico. Some materials, like shower liners, faucet fixtures and kitchen sinks are easier to get at Home Depot. We don't want to go over the permitted import amounts, so we tend to bring things down in small quantities, over lots of trips. That's just the beginning. After that we have to find someone reliable to do the construction, and it's helpful to be able to reach them by phone periodically.

    Russ and Bucky live in La Buf full-time. He built our kitchen, but the local plumber we hired to do the water lines only showed up sporadically, and not always when we were there to meet with him. I was the one delegated to communicate with him because my Spanish is fairly functional—but I could barely understand a word he said. He mumbled—in fast-forward. Then Russ' cell phone quit working. We have to prepay airtime for cell phones down in Baja—and it runs out fast. Every time I tried to call, a recording in Spanish would inform me that the number was not *disponible*, which means the phone was out of money.

    Okay, back to remodeling the kitchen. It was only supposed to take a month. It took three. We cleared everything out of our makeshift kitchen. We hauled the sink unit out to the patio. We stacked the couches on top of each other. We boxed up whatever wasn't already in boxes and piled everything around the edges of the living room. We jammed the stove and refrigerator in front and moved the rest of the stuff into the extra bedroom—so there would be enough room for Russ to work. Terry hooked a small propane bottle to the stove so we could still cook. The fridge was still plugged in. I did my best to put the boxes with our necessities (like coffee, cups, paper plates, utensils and a few canned goods) within reaching distance.

We left that weekend, thinking that by my birthday, three and a half weeks later, we'd waltz in, put everything away in my new cupboards, sweep the floor, dust a little and make ourselves right at home. We even planned a party for that Saturday night.

When we showed up, Russ was fairly far along—but nowhere near finished. We threw the party anyway. We were able to use the stove, the fridge, the barbecue and the outside sink with the hose. Luckily the weather cooperated, so everyone hung outside. Then, Russ took the month of October off to put a new roof on his own house before the rains came. We came down twice in October and it rained hard both times. There was nowhere to sit in our house, except on a bed or on the toilet. There were piles of sodden sawdust and construction stuff all over the patio. We couldn't bathe because the wall between the two bathrooms had been knocked down. I tried once, but when I turned on the hose, with no wall to act as a splashboard, the whole bathroom flooded! The water was too cold by then, anyway. I left swearing that I wouldn't return until the kitchen was done. Actually, I wasn't sure if I ever wanted to come back.

We stayed away for a month and a half. But when we returned, we forgot all the discomfort and mess in an instant. The metamorphosis from construction nightmare to Terry's and my dream kitchen took our breath away. In retrospect, it was all way worth it. But—you know—there was still the matter of the bathroom. The new shower (made of beach rock and glass block) wasn't ready yet. It was close, but there was still nowhere to bathe. Russ promised us that when we came down after Christmas, we'd be showering—in hot water.

Visions of my birthday weekend danced through my head as he said those words. For the next three weeks I fretted. What if it took six weeks, or two months to finish the shower and get the plumbing and propane lines in? Where was that plumber anyway? We couldn't find him. No one answered his phone. Again, I'd already invited too many people down for New Year's, bragging to them about our marvelous new kitchen and bathroom. We were going to be there a week. There were going to be too many of us to even attempt going around camp begging showers from the neighbors, like Gayle and Chelsea did in the summer. What would we do?

* * * *

Postscript:

Russ finished the shower by Christmas. There was no bathroom sink or vanity, but the toilet and shower were totally functional. Like all good Baja travelers, we just brushed our teeth and washed our faces in the kitchen ... all nine of us.

The sunset walk

Cactus Stock 21—A Backyard Music Bash in Baja
Summer 2001

On August 3rd and 4th I went to Cactus Stock—a weekend-long party on a lunar mountainside at the edge of the Pacific in Baja. About 500 people showed up. Musicians jammed in the afternoons on the cliffside stage—with the ocean a startling 150 feet below—their backdrop only sea, hills and sky. We parked ourselves under the shade of a eucalyptus tree and listened. Leaves rustled above me. My head was cool; my legs warm from the sun. Although I wouldn't have guessed it, some of these folks had never played in "public" before, and most had never played together. People wandered by, in shorts and bathing suits, sipping beers or bottles of water, checking it all out, even dancing now and then. We visited with old friends and made new ones. We hiked up and down hills, checking out the view from every different angle. Cars snaked up and down the twisted, steep road next to our campsite all day long. "Hey, you're here now, man. Be easy," called the guy next door to a pickup driving too fast and stirring up too much dust.

Cactus Stock. Intimate. Friendly. Mellow. The sticker they

passed out when people paid their entry fee read: "Music - Love - Peace." It was a party-friendly zone with the underlying attitude that it was not cool to be uncool. Sort of like a high school reunion—Baja style.

Only 20 minutes from La Bufadora, and just around the corner from Punta Banda, the landscape seemed from another world to me—the greens and blues of the sea a stark contrast to the steep, carved, almost-white cliffs that rose so dramatically above it. From above, we watched kayakers take off in groups of two to ten, paddling out to Zeppelin Rock—a long, low, guano-encrusted outcropping that stands guard at the entrance to the tiny bay, then north toward La Bufadora or south toward Los Arbolitos—darting through any one (or more) of at least a dozen volcanic arches dotting the coastline. I was outwardly sorry my kayak wasn't with me—but secretly glad not to have to haul it down and up that gnarly bluff. Overheated, dirty and sweaty by late Saturday afternoon, Terry and I made the trek down to the beach, climbed out onto the rocks and dove, hollering, into the crystal clear 58-degree ocean. I have a theory that the Fountain of Youth is right there, on the southern edge of Punta Banda. The water jars me. It refreshes me. No matter how hot and tired I am, it wakes me up. When I'm in it, I feel more alive than at any other time. The ocean is so clean and transparent that sometimes I can see my shadow below me on the ocean floor as I swim along.

A big part of being at Cactus Stock is making the traditional Sunset Walk (Hint: There is no level ground here, so every "walk" is really more of a hike.) to Crow's Point to cheer the sun as it settles into the horizon. At least 300 people made this walk on Friday and Saturday evenings. The camaraderie was magical; spirits were high. One of my favorite parts of the weekend was catching the moon as it rose up like a celestial pearl over the mountaintops, dazzling my eyes while strains of music and laughter drifted up the hillside. Afterward, each night there was dancing to North County (as in San Diego) bands playing surf music, ska, country swing, original creations, and rhythm and blues and classic rock until the wee hours of the morning. I never made it past 1:00 a.m. Sue boogied the night away—until after four—both nights.

Cactus Stock—love child of Encinitas residents Jimmy Joe Gooding and Miles Kenney—happens every year, usually in August. A full moon is required. It started out in the desert east of San Diego, near Ocotillo, back in 1987. There were two events a year at first. Cactus Stock 7 was in Julian, but it got too huge. About 1200 people showed up, and the preferred size is under 700. It was then that Miles and Jimmy Joe decided to try doing it in Mexico. Jimmy Joe knew the perfect place. They figured the logistics of getting there (the last couple of miles are on a somewhat tricky dirt road) and the rustic environment would keep the numbers down to a manageable level. Cactus Stocks 8, 9 and 10 were first known as Mex Stock 1, 2 and 3. By the time Cactus Stock 11 rolled around, the event was permanently moved south. There are other challenges beside the road. There's no electricity or running water at the Kennedy Ranch at Campo El Zeppelin. For this reason, there are far more guys than gals present.

When I asked them what motivated them to throw a party of this magnitude, they laughed. "I was playing in party bands in Del Mar," Miles told me. "But the cops always showed up after about the second song and broke up the parties. We got sick of it. I was studying geology at the time out in the desert and thought, 'Wow, all this land ... we should be playing out here.' I book the bands and Jimmy Joe takes care of everything else—getting the permits, having the road and campground graded, working with the Kennedy family (who owns the land), trucking in the generators and porta-potties, setting up the lights, maintaining the site and checking people in and out. It's a huge undertaking...." I can attest to that. My first morning there, as I staggered down the hillside at 8:30, coffee cup in hand, I ran into Jimmy Joe and his bride, Lisa. They were doing latrine duty—cleaning three of the many porta-potties. In true Baja style, they strung rolls of toilet paper onto rebar and duct taped them to the side of each unit, so that there would be no shortage of the stuff later on. Good move. Serious dedication.

This may have been the last festival to be held at Campo El Zeppelin. Estela Kennedy's family owns the land, and she's in the process of passing it on to her heirs. Jimmy Joe has been coming here for 18 years. He built a house here, in three phases—with leftover materials from his construction jobs. He also put together the stage for Cactus Stock here, poco a poquito. The first year that the event was held in Baja, there was no palapa, no stage and no dance floor. The generator was iffy. But by this year, which was the eleventh time the event was staged at Kennedy's; there was a main stage with a huge palapa, a dance floor and a second stage on the cliff. There was also

Estela's Cantina where revelers could buy mouth-watering tacos of fresh fish or carne asada, served on homemade tortillas with salsa made from just-picked produce from their farm.

This was actually my second time at Cactus Stock. I went three years ago too. Both times I have to say, it was an adventure ... an experience such as I haven't lived since the early '70s. But then, I'm not afraid of dirt. I'm not afraid to hold my breath when I use an outhouse. I'm not afraid to jump in the cold water in lieu of bathing. And I'm certainly not afraid to listen to great music played in a spectacular location ... with peaceful, happy people. I hope Cactus Stock lives on ... for many, many years.

It's a dog's life, again....

The Zippity Doo Dog from Tijuana Tells Her Tale
Fall 2001

"Hi there, people. My name is Cassie, also known as Cassandra (when I'm in the doghouse), Miss Wass and the Lover Dogette. Yes, I am a dog. A small, black and white Mexican dog, actually. I'm the second Baja dog to be adopted by Ann and Terry. They got me on June 1st, but it's taken me six months to get around to sharing my story with you. Why? Well ... because I was very shy. I'm just now starting to come out of my shell (to borrow a tide pool metaphor) and feel safe around humans. My English is also much better now.

"I was born in Tijuana about 14 months ago. My memory of my first few months is hazy. Like all children with painful, troubled pasts, I have chosen to block much of it out. It suffices to say ... I was a stray. My mom was a stray. She didn't have much milk and I was the only one of my siblings to make it through puppy hood. As soon as I grew teeth, it was off to the garbage cans to forage for food. That's how we lived. We were trash dogs. People didn't like us in their trash and threw rocks at us. Those memories still haunt me and I'm still afraid of new people—especially teenage boys. But I'm working on it. I'm just now beginning to learn the meaning of the word trust.

"You know, even though I'm more comfortable around humans now, and even though I'm getting used to having fresh food and water available at all times ... even though my life is about as close to perfect as a dog's life could get, I'm still a trash junkie. I have to admit this, or Ann would edit it in for me—I know she would. So … okay. True confession. I am still a trash dog. One whiff of a trashcan brimming over with paper, plastic, food scraps—pretty much anything munchable— and I lose control. As soon as no one is looking, I'll knock it over and begun spreading the contents all over the house (or garage, or back yard). I love to tear up cardboard and lick off any goodies still clinging to the pieces. I love to carry around empty milk jugs and chew the tops off. I love leftovers. Bones. Oh, yum! Dirty laundry too. Last night Ann put on a pair of Capri pants. She was going to a Water Polo meeting with Gayle. About ten minutes before leaving, she noticed a huge gaping hole in the right rear of her pants. (Now they're in the trash!) I was Cassandra at that moment. I was in the doghouse again. However ... in my own self-defense, I have to say that when I get to go to Doggy Beach at least every other day, I'm not nearly so inclined to go trash can diving. When I'm not bored and antsy, my self-control seems to be a lot stronger.

"Anyway, I digress. What I really wanted to tell you was how I came to live in the United States. Unlike my buddy, Gonzo, I wasn't just picked up off the beach and whisked away. Nope. I was sick. I was malnourished. I had mange. My left front leg was broken. It's still crooked, but I can run like the wind. In fact, another one of my nicknames is Zippity Doo Dog. I'm fast! And I can swim really well too. Better than Gonzo. I fetch balls. I play soccer. And I'm not one bit scared of all those big dogs at the beach. I love it there. It's my favorite place—this side of the border. But you better believe that I know enough to stay away from cars now. The broken leg taught me that much.

"I was rescued. This guy named Chris Tatum owns the Solana Beach Do-It-Yourself Dog Wash near here. He's my hero. He works with a man named Alex Ynigo, who has a ranch near Tijuana and has been saving Baja dogs for almost 30 years. That's where I went. I was only about five months old at the time, and very sick. There were almost 200 dogs there. A vet came and gave me shots. He gave me all kinds of other medicine too and helped my leg get better. After a couple of months, Chris brought me to the U.S. He was going to put me up for adoption. However, I was still too sick to even be spayed, so he took me back to Mexico. Eventually, I got well enough to be spayed. That hurt, but even before my stitches were out, I was back in Solana Beach. A few days later, Ann and Terry brought Gonzo in for a haircut. I was in a little pen with four other dogs. Ann came to look at me and I jumped up against the wire mesh and gave her my best, toothy grin. (I have a great smile!) It worked. She fell in love, bought me and took me home. I was the 158th Tijuana dog to be adopted from the Dog Wash.

"It wasn't all roses after that, though. The Dog Wash was the only safe, loving place I'd ever been. I ran away three times in the first two days. The first time I escaped from Ann's friend Kathy's house around the corner from the Dog Wash. I ran like crazy, found the back door and skidded across the floor. "Hola everyone. I'm home!" Ann came and got me. I tried to do it again, but some joggers caught me. My first trip to Doggy Beach, when they let me off the leash ... well, I bolted again. Ann found me for the third time, under some bushes along the Coast Highway. There were enough cars zooming by to convince me that perhaps I ought to stay put and give these humans a chance. Good move, Cass.

"So that's my story. I'm very happy here. I love my humans. Gonzo is the best buddy in the world. I love my trips to La Bufadora—where I can be as free as I was as a puppy—without any worries. I'm trustworthy now and will never run away again. If I can just get over this trashcan diving thing, I will be the absolute perfect dog. I promise...."

Another lousy sunset in paradise

The Cure for Boof Burnout
Winter 2002

You know what teenagers and toddlers have in common? You can't let them out of your sight for very long!

For eight years, I've gone to La Bufadora just about every other weekend. My kids practically grew up there. But they don't love it anymore. Mexico bores my high schoolers these days. It can't compete with track, water polo, swim team, biking to the beach, hanging out with friends, and going to movies ... even work. What's a mother to do? Going to Mexico with them is out of the question. Going without them is challenging, to say the least. I will never repeat Teenage Summer Camp. There has to be a responsible adult close at hand here at all times, because we all know teenagers aren't nearly as worldly-wise and mature as they think they are.

Luckily for me, I have Chuck and Christy who stay with them from time to time. But they're having a baby soon and will be entering another phase of life—one that doesn't include teenager sitting.

With all that in mind, and with a little of what I (ashamedly) call "September 11th-itis," I decided a few weeks ago that I should sell my Baja casa. You know, the one I searched for for-nearly-ever. The one I squatted in for months before being able to buy it. The one I actually bought while standing in the middle of a dirt road. The house on the edge of the bay with the million dollar view ... my Mexican dream home.

What was I thinking? I had a terminal case of Boof Burnout, I told people. It wasn't a place to relax and recharge my batteries anymore. Instead, I came home wiped out. Tired from too much trauma or too many houseguests. What happened? Well, first of all there were those unforgettable occasions this past summer when my (emergency only) Mexican cell phone would ring and I'd hear things like:

"Mommy! Terry's truck broke down on the way home from water polo. I'm stranded in El Cajon!" Did we know she was driving the truck to El Cajon? Not exactly. Her car was in the shop and it wasn't done in time. Was the truck repairable? Nope. We sold it for salvage. The water pump blew and fried the engine.

Another trip: "Mommy! Someone vandalized my car!" The car was in Julian. The tires were slashed. Would I please come arrange for a tow truck to get it home? Did I have a choice? Nope. Was she supposed to be in Julian? Nope.

On yet another trip I was bitten by a brown recluse spider. Not fun. Pat, who's a paramedic, broke the big orange blister and Sue scrubbed the wound with tequila and lime. A farfetched remedy for sure, but it stopped the poison from spreading. Then Pat gave me some meds in a tiny vial to use if the itching got too intense. I broke a tooth the next morning trying to open it. That afternoon I was in the dentist's chair getting that tooth pulled. At least it took my mind off the itching.

Oh yeah. I almost forgot. In June, Terry was backing into our driveway upon our arrival for a relaxing weekend with his old friends, Dennis and Susie. He backed over Gonzo. The dog (thankfully) has fully recovered ... but it was touch and go for about 10 days. Severely anxiety-provoking.

So. You get my drift. It was a not a good summer in La Bufadora. After September 11th, the border was a mess and I felt justified in not going down there anymore. It felt much safer and saner all around to stay close to home. This was not an easy decision for me to make. I mean, Baja is a hugely important part of my life—it's my passion. And I felt extremely guilty about avoiding my favorite place on earth. After all, tourism was way down in Baja since the terrorist attacks on the U.S. The major portion of my work involves promoting tourism in Baja. What was I thinking anyway?

I made an ad and put it on my website. The photos took my breath away. I listed the house on several Baja bulletin boards. I started fielding inquiries. I made a decision to go down the last weekend in January to clean out some personal things and put up the For Sale sign. Yes, I even made up the sign.

Five minutes after my arrival I changed my mind. What was I thinking? What kind of menopausal, paranoid, delusional thinking had overcome me? I spent the entire trip admitting my lunacy and retracting my decision. It was the best five days I've spent down there in years. Terry and I took more photos of more glorious sunsets than ever before. I was re-boofed. By that, I mean I fell in love with the place all over again. I never put the sign up. The ad is off my website. I'm now talking about adding that Sautillo tile on the floors, Mexican tile on the counter tops, building a fireplace in the living room and fixing the steps out front. And guess what? I discovered that my kids are relieved. They don't hate La Bufadora after all. In fact, they can't wait 'til they're old enough to go down there ... without us.

Go figure.

Leslie, A Five-Star Houseguest, with Terry

How To Be a Five-Star Houseguest

If you have a house in Mexico you are going to have house-guests. It comes with the territory. Some people are subtle. They drop hints when looking for invitations. "You going to La Buf anytime soon? God, but I love it down there." Others offer their services—usually construction-oriented. "Say. I have some leftover tile from a job. Can you use it? I'll haul it down for you." The more desperate ones are the most blatant. "When are you going to invite me to your house? I'm free just about any weekend...." It's almost impossible to sneak a weekend away without someone (or three or more) tagging along. If we want alone time, we actually have to avoid telling our friends that we're leaving.

Debbie, Steve, Kim, Terry and I were sitting around our La Buf kitchen table one night not too long ago. We decided to make a list of what houseguests should do if they want to get invited back. We came up with ten ways to be a "Five-Star Houseguest:"

- You must be over 40. Or 35. We're not sure. Just no born again teenagers.
- You must stop at Duty Free on the way into Mexico and buy your own booze and cigarettes ... or buy them here ... unless you don't partake of either, of course.

- You can't have more fun than we do. It's illegal.
- You must be able to fall with grace. Most gringos are used to walking on concrete or asphalt. Dirt roads can be slippery, especially at night. And our stairs ... well ... they can be treacherous.
- You must have first aid capabilities—especially on First Night in Camp. Chiropractors (like Debbie) who provide free services are highly regarded.
- You must cook, do dishes, remember to put the toilet paper in the basket, flush when appropriate and learn how to take a Navy shower. You will be forgiven if cooking mishaps occur—such as the time Chuck was cooking a Thanksgiving turkey on a Weber grill and dropped it in the dirt. We hosed it off and ate it anyway—gritty as it was.
- If you stay more than three days, you must have at least one profound moment.
- You must be able to blow the conch shell, or at least try.
- If you want to stay an extra day, you must come up with a really good excuse. True excuses, like breaking a tooth and having to go to the dentist, beat out all whoppers. However, most of us have come up with inventive stories—stretching the truth or making up totally fictional excuses—to stay an extra day. These are preferable. The more creative the whopper, the better.
- Finally, if you really, really want to be invited back, paint a wall, wash the windows, weed or perform some other type of manual labor. Indentured service is mandatory.

* * * *

Houseguests often bring, what I call, "hostess gifts." They are not mandatory, but we have received a variety of them, usually purchased at the Mall.

My college roommate, Laurie, brought down my favorite hostess gift. She came with an almost-full bottle of very expensive tequila. The tequila was superb, and the bottle was made of hand-blown Mexican glass with a green rim around the top. It had a cork and a wood stopper. At the bottom of the bottle was a tiny green glass agave plant. It's usable art. I scrubbed the label off and we keep it on the counter to use as a decanter. Laurie went to the Mall and found a shot glass that matched perfectly. So that sits next to the bottle.

Laurie also gave us a pair of really huge stainless steel bowls. She knows I cook for crowds there more often than not, so she knew I'd use them. What was even more amazing than the utility of the gift was that her bowls nested perfectly with the stainless steel bowls I already had—and matched too.

Amy's not a houseguest. She's a neighbor who comes over for dinner a lot. She always brings something. She gave us a set of yellow ceramic bowls to match the kitchen, a couch, and a turquoise shell bath mat. She loaned us a banquet table to use before we had a kitchen. She always brings food too. The last time she was over she left behind an art deco appetizer tray in just my colors. I washed it and put it in the cupboard. Do you think she'll forget it's there, so I can keep it? I'm crossing my fingers.

Then there are the houseguests (they're definitely the majority) who shop at the Mall. They come back with clay suns and moons to hang on the wall, cherubs or other statuettes, pieces of stained glass, candles and candleholders. We have them all over the place.

The most hilarious hostess gift I ever received was from Debbie. She'd just had Thanksgiving dinner at her house the day before she arrived. In addition to turkey, dressing, cranberry sauce and pies, she brought me this little wooden turkey napkin holder with matching orange and brown napkins. I bet her mom gave it to her. It doesn't go with my Mexican folk art theme, so I'm planning on recycling it next year. Hopefully I'll get invited to her house and I can give it back. It can become an annual tradition.

Part Three: People, Places and Adventures Along the Way

An agave in bloom

Can You Tell Me ...Where is the Second World?
... En El Corazón Mexicano

Whenever I get ready to head south, I find myself wondering a lot about the first and third worlds. At this point, the inevitable question that ricochets around my mind is: "Exactly where is the second world?"

We have the first. We have the third. To me, the first world is where corporate giants rule and technology is god. It's a place where we have identical tract homes with fresh paint, new furniture, at least three cordless phones, TV sets with VCRs or DVDs, computers with modems, cable or DSL hookups. It's a place where our shiny, new, leased SUVs and mini-vans stack up bumper to bumper on freeways and on surface streets that get more crowded every year. Tall buildings dominate the skyline and sunsets are often tinged with burnt orange from smog.

We have insurance to cover every inevitable mishap, yet when one occurs, we have to fight for months to get our insurance companies to pay up. With the exception of our inner cities, the first world is remarkably sanitary. Pretty much everything is paved and even rivers flow in concrete ditches. Our fenced, manicured yards prevent dogs from wandering. Automatic sprinklers water our lawns. We can buy everything we need to eat at Vons, Smart and Final or Costco and use our microwave ovens to whip up instant meals in minutes. Very few of us cook, garden or sew anymore.

When we think of the third world, the images that come to mind are starkly different. We think of ignorance, overpopulation, government corruption and the huge gap between the wealthy and the poor. We think of narrow, paved roads full of potholes, with decaying dog carcasses and trash scattered randomly along the edges. Or dirt roads where a film of dust covers every slow moving beat up car that wanders by with at least one headlight out. Buildings are painted in vibrant, random shades of magenta, turquoise, orange and cobalt blue—when they're painted at all. Color rules. Music blares. Streets bustle as neighbors and families share in each other's hardships, struggles and triumphs. Open spaces are far more prevalent than urban sprawl, but that makes us gringos nervous—because this world is foreign to us—not only in terms of language and culture, but also because it's still raw, chaotic and has a wild frontier spirit that feels ready to burst forth at any second. We're afraid of the dirt, the poverty, the drugs and crime (and we don't have those?). We're uncomfortable with the disparity between this other world and the one we take for granted ... and we considers ours far superior.

So why did the spin-doctors label us a first world country and our neighbor to the south, Mexico, a third world country? Again, where is the second world?

Because I bounce back and forth between the two countries, I have some thoughts on that subject. To me, the second world is a blending of the other two. But it's sort of invisible—like a state of mind. You can't see it or touch it or quantify it by rigid standards—at least not our standards. Affluence is not the ultimate goal in life—but neither is poverty acceptable.

No. The second world is a place of simplicity and contentment. It's a place where materialism and one-upmanship rank far below friendship, cooperation, helpfulness and kindness. Where fear—whether it's of being mugged, cheated, outmaneuvered or outdone is not at the forefront of everyone's mind. Have you seen the movie, *Pay it Forward*? I think that kid invented the second world.

Does it exist outside a movie theater? For me it does. I find it south of the border—in a supposed third world country. But I think it's anywhere people really care about each other. For me, it helps too if there's fresh air and elbowroom—and if the beauty of the natural world dominates the landscape.

I find it in little fishing villages scattered along the Gulf of California, where the locals share their bounty with anyone who happens to show up, whether it's by land or sea. Where the Americans who intrude give back gifts of whatever they have on hand, in gratitude for the food, music and friendship they receive. I find it in the *Norte Americanos* who've settled into Baja to spend their retirement years with a view of the pounding surf in a home they could never afford in Alta California. These folks have become a part of their communities. They spend their money locally. They participate in fiestas of all kinds—from *quincineras* (15 year old girls' coming out parties) to weddings, funerals and religious holidays. They gather money from their neighbors when anyone, be it a local or another expatriate, is in need of financial help. They share.

I find the second world also in the hearts of the Mexicans who embrace us and encourage us as we struggle with our ragged Spanish. I relate to the Americans who flee our country so they can live in less crowded places with neighbors who are their friends, and who understand the concept of live and let live. They are eager to downsize and reduce their earthly possessions to a more manageable, uncomplicated level. They move south in search of a more comfortable, considerate and gentle lifestyle, away from our consumer society. To me—that is the second world.

If I believe everything the media tells me, people in third world countries desire nothing more than to catapult into the first world. There are some who do yearn northward, toward the gleaming skylines of San Diego, who long for affluence and all the goodies money can buy. But what if they were offered another option—the second world—a place without the constant clawing and grappling of the first world and the privation of the third; a place where people look out for one another, refusing to bow to corporate gods of technology and relentless Darwinism. Where people strive to live in harmony with one another, and with the earth. I've seen it. I've felt it. I wish more people could, because I think we'd all be an awful lot happier—somewhere between first and third. That's where I hope President Fox will take Mexico ... to the forefront of the second world—to model for the world a country whose values include respect, friendship, tolerance, generosity, openness and accountability—for all living creatures and for the planet we inhabit. I call this *corazón*—heart.

This section of Agave Sunsets is about traveling in Baja (with one side trip to the Mayan Riviera to visit an old Boof buddy). It focuses on the people, places and adventures along the way. These stories demonstrate to me the beauty, simplicity and whimsical nature of the second world.

Ann, Nina and friends with John

PEOPLE....

John Bragg—The Tequila Man

John Bragg has the largest known tequila collection in the world. At last count (spring, 2002) he had over 500 different types of tequila, pulque and mezcal. Since 1990, he and his wife Mary and have owned and managed Pancho's Restaurant and Tequila Bar in Cabo San Lucas. When I met them on a trip to Baja Sur back in 1997, we hit it off immediately. They invited my group to dinner at their restaurant, and after we ate, John treated us to one of his tequila tastings. Because tequila is not only the fruit of the agave, but truly "the essence of Mexico," I think it's only fitting that I pass on some of John's knowledge (which is as extensive as his collection). According to him, tequila isn't for the timid—it's for those of us who, like the Mexicans, are passionate, strong and warmhearted—people who live life with gusto. While most Norte Americanos think of tequila as something to be tossed back with a dash of salt and a lime, or added into a Margarita, serious tequila drinkers are slow, thoughtful sippers. This is because tequila—like no other liquor—has a delayed reaction. It catches the uninitiated off-guard.

The Mayans started it all, way before the Spaniards showed up. Their fermented beverage of choice was pulque (pool-KAY), which they made from the agave mezcalero. It was used primarily for medicinal and religious purposes. In those days, drunkenness was a crime punishable by death and only old people and nursing mothers were given free access to pulque. Why? Because of its tranquilizing effects and high nutritional value. To this day, Indians still mix home-made pulque into their herbal medicines to treat diseases. There are still *pulquerías*—pulque bars—in various parts of Mexico. However, they're definitely not for the faint-hearted or for the ladies, because a pulquería generally has no restroom—just a trough on the floor in the back of the room. The women buy pulque through a window off the street.

When the conquistadors and missionaries arrived in Mexico, they tried pulque, but at 30% alcohol, it wasn't strong enough for their liking. They began experimenting with the agave mezcalero and came up with mezcal. Then they experimented with distilling different varieties of agave, and eventually created tequila. The plant tequila is made from is the blue agave, or the Agave Tequilana Weber and is considered the most exceptional of all agaves because it produces the most full-bodied, clean-tasting liquor. And it's all—every ounce of it—produced within 100 miles of Guadalajara, in central Mexico. Today, over 90,000 acres of blue agave are cultivated in this region, with the greatest number of fields near the small city of Tequila, about 45 miles northeast of Guadalajara. It's home to 20 distilleries—*fábricas* in Spanish—that produce over 55 million liters of tequila per year. The Tequila Man and Mary now live most of the year nearby—in Ajijic. No wonder he's such an expert.

When a plant is mature, at between seven and ten years old, it shoots a flower-bearing stalk as high as 15 feet in the air. The dramatic yellow bloom will last a month or so, but it signals the agave's impeding demise, for it dies soon after. The agave on this cover bloomed the year before, so it's past its prime—but still dramatic. Right before the stalk emerges is harvest time. Field workers remove the agave's core, called the piña, carry it to the fábrica where it's split in half and cooked in a large oven—*horno*—for about 24 hours. After cooling another 24 hours, the piñas are crushed, strained, mixed with water and put in large vats to ferment. After fermenting for 72 to 150 hours, the liquid is filtered and put into stills. The distillation process is carried out twice, and the final product emerges at 100 to 120 proof. It's then diluted with distilled water until it reaches the proper range of 76 to 90 proof.

There are three types of tequila. The first is a *blanco* or *joven*. (HOE-ven, which means young). A joven is only aged one or two additional months. The second is a *reposado* (which means rested), which is aged in wood for three to 12 more months. John claims that, "A really good reposado grabs you by the throat and gently lets go." The third type of tequila, *añejo* (Ahn-YAY-hoe, which means vintage) has been aged at least a year. Tequila ages quickly, so one that's five or six years old is considered *"muy añejo,"* or very old.

When we did our tasting, most of us preferred the blanco. John served us one called Don Juan and if you want to try your hand at some thoughtful, slow tequila sipping, this is definitely one to choose, or Don Julio which is another favorite of ours. Or try Terry's and my current favorite—Hornitos. It's a reposado and a little more affordable.

John has a parting thought he'd like to leave with you. "If you come to Pancho's in Cabo with a bottle of unopened tequila, and it's one I don't have in my collection, I'll buy the bottle from you and your dinner will be on the house—even if I'm not there!"

Togo Hazard, Chuy Valdez and Steve Chism

Expatriated Americans
... or ...
As the Palapa Turns, Down East Cape Way

Since my 20s I've fantasized about living in Mexico—not just for a few months out of the year—but for good. I'm perennially envious of those expatriates I've met in Baja (and elsewhere) who've sold everything in the States and just up and flown the coop.

Why do they do it? They do it for a million different reasons—but mostly because they can't help themselves. Something deep inside an expatriate relaxes once he or she finds that perfect spot on the planet. The simpler lifestyle, closer to the whims and moods of Mother Nature, beckons. Instead of being stuck inside a cubicle, a car or a condo ... you can live on the beach, or within sight of it. The lack of pretense beckons too. In Baja you can reinvent yourself. You can be whoever and whatever you want to be—as long as you're cool about it. It doesn't matter if you were a banker, a truck driver or a drywall hanger in your previous life. In Baja, you're accepted for you. The labels are left behind—with the three-piece suits and the pantyhose.

The expatriates I've known over the years have something else in common. They're almost uniformly eccentric—in one way or another. Check out some of the synonyms for this word and you'll pretty much have a rundown on the cast of characters you'll find living in the outposts of Baja. How about this: kook, nut, oddball, rugged individualist, renegade, nonconformist, freak, maverick, and weirdo. Expatriates all pretty much march to the beat of their own inner drummers ... and they like living somewhere where their idiosyncrasies are not merely put up with, but applauded.

One of my favorite expatriates is Steve Chism. He's about 10 years older than I am and lives in Los Barriles, near the Hotel Buena Vista Beach Resort where he's worked since 1981. He has (at least) eight dogs. He has really long gray hair and a really long gray beard. He's wiry, he's funny and he's a walking encyclopedia. He spends a good part of every day during fishing season in a little shack right on the beach in front of the hotel, repairing fishing gear and renting masks, snorkels and fins, jet skis, ATVs and kayaks to the hotel patrons. Most of the time, he's reading. He has a library in that beach shack that boggles the mind. It includes vintage Baja books, maps, and books on the area's history, its geography, birds, plant life and fish. He knows them all inside out.

I met him early (make that way too early) on a cold, blustery February morning in 1982. I was with my boyfriend at the time. It was my first trip to Cabo and it was super windy the whole time. But we wanted to go fishing and my dad had told us about this new hotel, the Spa. He said to go in and ask for Steve, and for sure we'd get a fishing boat. There were no phones in Buena Vista until 1995, so they had no clue that we were coming. In those days, all reservations were made through a stateside office and the information was snail-mailed to the Valdez family in La Paz. We could've called their stateside number before we left, but my dad assured us that just mentioning his name would open all the right doors and grease all the wheels that needed to be greased. So, on that recommendation, we got up before dawn and made the hour-long drive to the East Cape. We got there in time for breakfast. I found Steve.

"Hi," I said. "I'm Togo Hazard's daughter. He said you could get us a boat."

Steve gave me a withering look. "Who?"

I back-peddled. "Togo Hazard. He's a good friend of Chuy's."

Another one of those looks. I kept on. "You know, the owner of this hotel. My dad comes here once or twice a year with a huge group of construction guys to fish."

Third withering look. "Sorry. Never heard of him." He turned and walked away.

Boy, did I feel stupid, but I wasn't giving up. "Wait," I said, tugging at his arm. "Can we get a boat anyway?"

It was a lousy day for fishing, so of course we got a boat. I've never been on seas as rough as those—ever. Thankfully, I didn't get seasick, but I couldn't sit down either. I had to stand up, my legs braced against the side of the boat, and I had to hang on with both hands. I had to use the tiny head in the cabin at one point. Just getting down in there was a challenge. Sitting on that toilet was like an "E Ticket" ride (back when they had E tickets) at Disneyland. The fish were not biting. We were desperate to catch something, however. Our *capitán*—captain—took us to the north end of *Bahía las Palmas*—Las Palmas Bay—and let us troll right offshore. My boyfriend caught a needlefish—skinny as a pencil, less than two feet long and good for absolutely nothing—not even bait. But it was a fish, right?

I've gotten to know Steve a lot better in the last two decades. Now we laugh about that first encounter. Over the years, as the hotel grew, he's worn a lot of different sombreros. He ran the boats for a while. After that, he helped check guests in and out. I can vouch for the fact that he is the person most responsible for transforming an expanse of naked sand into the lush oasis that is now the hotel grounds. I saw him planting purple, pink and red bougainvillea, hibiscus and oleander several years back. I saw him coordinating the workers as they planted coconut palms, aloe and grass. Over the years fountains sprang up—some with dramatic metal sculptures of flying fish, some with cherubs. Steve found his niche. This was and is a place he could study, work and create beauty from nothingness. These days, the hotel is magnificent, with a swim-up bar and plenty to offer guests like me, who come for something other than world-class sport fishing.

In the off-season, during the winter, Steve and his expatriate buddies go four wheeling. Sometimes he goes solo; sometimes they travel in groups as large as 20. Most of the time they have a destination in mind. As Steve told me, "Sometimes that works and sometimes it doesn't. We've been to ranchos that have existed for 200 years or more and operate much the same as they did back then. We've seen tame deer, quail, playful raccoons and a flock of ostriches. We've also been to gold mines, Indian cave paintings and kitchen midden sites, and seen more streams and waterfalls than you'd believe exist in these mountains."

These guys have traveled up and down both coasts of Baja Sur and through the mountains that separate them. As he said, these mountains are surprisingly full of water. There are stone pools big enough to swim in year-round. Palms and *jueribos*—similar to cottonwood trees, line the banks of these streams. There really are orchards and farms latticed along the mountainsides where families nurture livestock and grow tropical fruits, just as their ancestors have for generations. And all of this in a land that looks from the air to be utterly barren and devoid of life.

My favorite of Steve's Baja stories is the one about the ladder. The way he tells it, he and his buddy, Dewaine took off late one afternoon and headed up an arroyo toward the mountains on their ATVs. When they couldn't drive any further, they got off and started climbing up through a field of boulders. After picking their way through a dense palm grove, they found themselves in an orchard. There were oranges, tangerines, grapefruit, papaya, avocados, guava, mangos and sugar cane. And even more amazing—there was a drip irrigation system! They helped themselves to a couple of grapefruits. Dewaine picked a dozen or so to take home and left behind a half-empty bottle of tequila as a thank you gift.

They visited the orchard off and on throughout the winter. Each time, they'd take fruit and leave a bottle of tequila, whiskey or vodka behind. According to Steve, "One day, Dewaine went by himself. He ran into an old man up on a rickety wooden ladder picking fruit. He introduced himself, told the old man what he'd been doing over the past few months and offered to pay for the fruit he'd taken. The old man told him that he was welcome to take as much fruit as he wanted. His family couldn't eat it all, and they had no way to get it down the mountain to market. He didn't even have a ladder tall enough to get the fruit off the top branches.

"The next time Dewaine went stateside, he bought an 18-foot orchard ladder. The following December, a few of the guys moved the ladder up to the orchard and propped it against a tree so the old man would find it.

"In late January, Dewaine told me he thought maybe the old man was dead. 'Why?' I asked. 'Because I haven't seen him all winter and I'm the only one using the orchard ladder.'" Steve chuckled. "One day he went up there and ran into the old man. He was on top of the rickety old ladder picking fruit. You have to understand. This old ladder wasn't just rickety; it was damned dangerous! My buddy asked the old man why he wasn't using the new ladder. 'It's a fine ladder,' he said. 'But it isn't mine, señor!'"

There's another punch line to this story too, believe it or not. One night (whether it was before or after the last incident, I don't know) Dewaine was at Mañana's Pizza Parlor in Los Barriles having dinner. The waitress came over to him and shook her head at him. "I see you've been to my grandfather's again," she said.

"How do you know that?" he asked.

"Because he's drunk."

"KiKi" Rolle

A Hockey Player from Minnesota
Running a Spanish School in Baja?
Since 1997

That's right. There's a hockey player from Minnesota running
a Spanish immersion school in Ensenada. Honest. When I first heard
of Keith Rolle, my friends at Discover Baja Travel Club told me that
he was someone I had to meet. It was about four years ago and Keith
had just opened his school. I emailed him and invited him to a party at
Nina's house in La Buf. He showed up, introduced himself and we hit
it off immediately.

But how did he get from being a bigwig with Toro, the lawn
mower superpower in Minneapolis to running *Colegio de Idiomas de
Baja California*—the Baja California Language College? Well, like all
good expatriates, Keith's got a renegade heart. A few years ago he
found that in his travels with Toro, more and more people he did business with spoke Spanish. He was fluent in French, but that wasn't
doing him much good in Mexico. He heard about a school in
Ensenada that offered weeklong Spanish immersion programs and
signed up for two weeks' worth. The company paid, of course. Then he
went back again for another three weeks. By then, he was hooked on

Ensenada. He was also hooked on the idea of starting his own school.

He quit his high-paying job, started up a Mexican corporation and moved to San Diego, where he commutes back and forth to Ensenada. Keith has a team of six instructors, and another eight on standby who come in when a huge group of students shows up. The classes are small—with no more than five people per teacher. Nearly everyone who comes to the school stays with a Mexican family. It's part of the immersion process. "They eat, sleep, drink and live in Spanish," Keith says. "For the first thee days it's real hard. Then, by the fourth day, there's always a breakthrough as they start to feel more confident."

"If Terry and I come, can't we stay in La Bufadora and commute?" I asked him once. "No," was the emphatic response. "Living with a Mexican family is an invaluable part of the experience. Host families are selected for their friendliness, willingness to assist people with their studies, and for their superior accommodations. They're all middle class families in comfortable homes with all the amenities we're accustomed to."

I asked if we could stay together. Another emphatic no. "You won't learn as fast if you're together because you'll speak English to each other." Good point. I was nearly fluent once—in 1970 when I spent a summer in Spain. I even had a Spanish boyfriend who spoke no English. That was motivating, for sure. As I remembered the incredible feeling I got from being able to communicate easily in Spanish (*ya no más*—not anymore), I was immediately reminded of something a Mexican friend told me. Once she began dreaming in English, her teacher told her, she'd know she was really fluent. I don't know if I've ever dreamed in Spanish—but I will someday. These days, my Spanish varies from iffy to okay—depending on its mood. I haven't yet had the chance to spend a week or more at Keith's school, but that's because of my maternal responsibilities. I will though, I keep promising him.

So, who comes to the Baja Language College? Business executives, from the U.S., Canada and Europe. Teachers. Attorneys. Doctors. Human Resources professionals. Seniors. Families. Even kids. Anyone with a need or a passion to communicate in Spanish.

Obviously, the surge of foreign business investment in Mexico brought on by NAFTA has created a need for people working in Mexico to become bilingual. Most managers from the U.S. and

Canada working in Mexico don't speak Spanish. Although interpreters are typically available, there's nothing more effective than one-on-one communication. With Keith's program, not only do business people learn Spanish, but through immersion, they become familiar with the Mexican culture. Once they're able to actually talk to their Mexican associates, they have an even greater opportunity to pick up on the cultural differences in how business is conducted here.

I'm always impressed when I hang out with Keith in Ensenada. Everywhere we go, people know him. The bartenders in Hussongs joke and jive with him. He bowls every month with a group of local businessmen. They call him, "El Vikingo," for the Viking. Those who can't pronounce Keith just call him Kiki. He's easy going, funny and smart as hell. He fits in. The Mexicans not only respect him, but they have a good time with him.

So do I. Recently, we were among several designated speakers at Ensenada Appreciation Day. The program was running a little long, so Tillie, the organizer, asked us if we wanted to forfeit our speaking spots. I had an idea. "How about if we go up together?" I asked Keith. "Everyone in this room knows us. It's stuffy in here and people are looking pretty sleepy after two slide shows. Maybe we can wake them up with a little comic relief."

He had another idea. "How about if I'm you and you're me?"

So ... Keith introduced himself as Ann and started plugging my books. He did fine 'til he got to *Cartwheels*. "It's the story of three women who...."

I stuck four fingers in his face. "Oops. Four." Everyone cracked up.

When it was my turn, he wanted to make sure I let everyone know he'd just expanded his programs to include classes in basic Spanish for retirees—in places like Cantamar and San Felipe. So I gave the spiel. However, my brain short-circuited. "Hey Keith," he said to me. "You left out Loreto."

The Baja Animal Shelter

Saving Baja Dogs and Cats ... A Portrait of Devotion Since 1996

It would be an understatement to call Sunny Benedict a dog and cat lover. She's actually Baja California's premier pet activist. Anyone who travels in Mexico can't help but notice the large number of dogs lying dead on the side of the road, or the mangy, skinny strays wandering around—often females with drooping teats and downcast eyes.

In 1992, the first year Sunny lived in Rosarito, everyone she met complained about the stray dogs. However, no one seemed to have the time or energy to do anything about them. The situation disturbed her greatly, so she began to investigate. What she learned changed her life. Back in 1993 there were no animal shelters in northern Baja. There were (and still are) two *perreras*—dog pounds—one in Tijuana and another in Ensenada. An average of 60 dogs per day were (and are) put down at the Tijuana perrera. According to Sunny, this can be attributed to the low number of veterinarians cooperating with the perrera's low cost neuter and spay program, as well as the area's large population of unwanted animals.

Historically, dogs at the perreras have been electrocuted. Sunny has been encouraging them to use Phenobarbital instead. She told me,

"Fifteen dollars-worth of Phenobarbital would painlessly euthanize 30 large dogs. Although the Tijuana perrera does not have the budget to afford this, they're considering it and currently looking for funding." Lately she has been able to save four or five dogs a week in Tijuana ... but that's not enough.

In 1996, after she learned all this, Sunny put an ad in the *Baja Sun*, the local Rosarito newspaper, asking anyone interested in helping save strays to meet with her. Eighteen people showed up one night, chipped in $10 apiece and did some brainstorming. They had a fundraiser the following month, which netted $1,000. "After that," she said, "it was like a fast-moving train." It took a year to get the paperwork filed in Mexico City. In March of 1997 she received her nonprofit license in Mexico. She found a piece of land to rent for $300 a month in the hills behind Rosarito and began taking in strays. On any given day you can find 300 to 350 dogs and cats at her shelter. Last time I was there she had over 400. Of the 4,000 pets she's rescued, about 2,000 have been adopted—98% of these in the United States. However, some obviously didn't make it. We met Pitufas, a Chihuahua puppy, who'd come in a few weeks earlier with her mom and four siblings. They'd all been living on the streets, were weak, starving and dehydrated. All died but Pitufas, who wasn't out of the woods yet when we visited. While we were there, Sunny fed her vitamins to bolster her immune system, and cough medicine for a respiratory infection. She made it; she was one of the lucky ones.

Sunny has a tight, dedicated network of volunteers in the States. Pet stores help her with adoptions. Any pets that aren't adopted at the U.S. events are placed in local foster care, where they stay until they find a home. Recently, two of Sunny's benefactors from Solana Beach bought her a parcel of raw land in Bonsall to use as an adoption facility. She hopes to build a facility that will house 20 dogs and up to 20 cats. This will eliminate the need for foster care. Her volunteers can pick up the animals and take them to adoption events. The public will be able to walk in and visit with pets they're looking to adopt. She also envisions caretaker quarters, and a small clinic to provide minor treatments, as soon as she finds volunteers who can help with the funding, design and construction.

"We make sure all animals are vaccinated, wormed, spayed and neutered," Sunny explains. "Puppies and kittens are fixed at three months old. We don't send any animal north of the border to be adopted until it's healthy. We have a seven-day guarantee period too. If an adoption doesn't work out within a week or so, the family can call our foster care people. They'll come pick up the pet and refund the adoption fee.

"The Baja Animal Sanctuary does not use euthanasia as a means of population control," Sunny assured me. "The only animals we put down are the ones who are too sick or injured to have a decent quality of life. I have about 20 dogs at my shelter that will never be adopted. They're just here. They hang out." I saw them. They have good lives.

"How much does it cost to run an operation like this?" I asked. Well, the dogs eat 300 pounds of food per day in the summer, and about 400 pounds per day in the winter. The shelter has 10 full-time employees, two of whom stay overnight. There's no electricity, so when the sun goes down they have to fire up a gas generator. Water is trucked in daily and is a major expense, as is neutering and spaying. Fortunately, several U.S.-based vets donate medications, but the need always exceeds the budget.

It can't be easy. The entire operation runs on donations. "I remember one nasty winter day," she told me. "There was no food. No money in the bank. It was cold. I sat down in the dirt and 20 dogs circled me, licking me. I looked up to the sky and cried out, 'God, where's the food?' All of a sudden, a bright red jeep with Arizona plates drove up. They'd heard about me, they said. They wanted to help. So they'd loaded up their vehicle with dog food and drove here." She smiled. "Every time I get discouraged, something surprising and wonderful happens."

She goes on. "I have the licensing ability to open animal shelters all over Mexico. Other communities need to get together and build their own shelters, otherwise all the dogs will end up in the perreras. I can help them get started, but I can only run this one. It's a seven-day-a-week job."

To me, Sunny is a hero. I am a pet lover too. But she's only one person trying to solve a huge problem. There are only two humane societies in all of Baja that I'm aware of. Hers is one. The other is in Cabo San Lucas. Another friend of mine, Janet Howey is trying to open a shelter in Todos Santos, and I'm sure there are other quiet heroes around, like Chris Tatum from Solana Beach Do-It-Yourself Dog Wash, who are dedicated to saving Mexican dogs.

Derek's 302-pound Marlin

The "Spa" Turns 25
Halloween 2001

Every trip south weaves its own reality. No two are exactly the same. You never know whom you'll run into that you know, and whom you'll come away knowing that you didn't know before. It doesn't matter if it's Rosarito, La Bufadora or the East Cape, but you can bet your bottom peso that if you go to the same place in Baja year after year after year, you will always run into someone you hung out with before. And ... you will always make new friends. The Spa is definitely one of those places. It's a resort. People go to play. It's also one of those places where it's nearly impossible to keep to yourself and not meet everyone else. It's just too friendly and too intimate.

We flew down there—my dad, Terry and I—on Halloween, to celebrate the Hotel Buena Vista Beach Resort's 25th anniversary. It was my first time on a plane since the September 11th tragedy. I was a little afraid to fly, but once airborne, I forgot everything but the clarity of the day and the beauty of the world below me. I had the window seat, of course. Terry hates it that I always get the window seat, but why not? He offers. I accept. He complains. I gloat. We flew out of San Diego to the west and turned south, crossed the border and hugged the coastline from Tijuana to the border of Baja California Sur. I pointed out landmarks to Terry, and he leaned forward in his seat, craning his neck toward the window.

"I can't see shit," was all he said. Then he went back to his magazine.

It didn't deter me. My dad was in the aisle seat, and so I shouted over to him. "Dad, check this out. I can see La Bufadora! It's so clear that I can see the kelp in the bay. I can see the road leading up to our house. I can see everything!" My dad doesn't hear well. He didn't have a clue what I was going on about. He just smiled and went back to reading his book. It annoyed Terry, though—even more. He unbuckled his seat belt, stood up, leaned over me and pressed his face onto the window. He saw, finally.

We flew southward. I could see the Gulf of California to my left. I could see what looked to be Laguna Ojo de Liebre on the right. It was huge—much larger than I expected. The salt flats surrounded it. But where was Guerrero Negro? How could a city that large not show up from the air? I sneaked a peek at Axel. He had the window seat right in front of me. He was awake. Apparently, he didn't sleep on planes either. His brother, Esaul was slumped in his seat—out cold—and had been since about two minutes after takeoff. Of course, he's made this trip about a million times anyway. (In case you've forgotten, Axel and Esaul are Chuy Valdez' two oldest sons. Esaul manages the hotel. Axel manages the Stateside business and promotions.)

"Hey, Axel, where's Guerrero Negro?" I asked, tapping his shoulder and pointing out the window. He showed me. He also pointed out San Ignacio Lagoon just below it. As we turned east, Terry was the first to see mainland Mexico across the Gulf. Then we flew over La Paz, Isla Espiritú Santo and down the coast, past the East Cape and on toward Los Cabos. As we descended into the airport, we skimmed over the tops of the mountains. They looked close enough to reach out and touch. After the intense rains of Hurricane Juliette a month prior, they were an intense, dark green. There were deep sand washes on the lowlands where the water had poured from the mountains and rushed to the ocean. The desert was alive with color—the giant cardón were draped in green vines and splashed with yellow and magenta flowers. It's always a tropical thorn forest this time of year after the late summer rains—but I'd never seen it after a hurricane before. The untamable forces of nature were clearly painted on and etched onto the landscape below me.

On this trip, we met a group of 14 women from Portland, Oregon who called themselves the "Baja Babes." They weren't there for the anniversary celebration. They were on their annual trip—without men—to hang out, party their tail feathers off, and eventually, after they wore themselves out—to recharge their batteries. More about them later....

On Saturday Terry and I rented a car and made the loop north and west to the La Paz cutoff, then south on Highway 19 to Todos Santos. En route we stopped in Los Barriles to check out new Baja author, Jimmy Smith's book-signing. I'd never met him before, but had heard rumors that he loved to make fun of my book, *Cartwheels in the Sand*—telling his listeners that it was a flighty tale of four menopausal broads bickering their way through Baja. So, obviously I was somewhat apprehensive about meeting him. We found him eating breakfast with friends in front of the bookstore. I walked up with two copies of his book and asked for an autograph. As he was signing I mentioned, "By the way, Jimmy ... I'm Ann Hazard. Does that ring a bell?"

He jumped out of his chair, knocking it over. He upended his coffee cup too, spilling coffee all over the table and onto the sidewalk. Ignoring all that, he gave me a huge hug and kiss. "It is you! I've always wanted to meet you, you ol' broad!"

We talked a while, and he couldn't have been nicer. He asked when we'd be back from Cabo, and I said the next day. "Well, then. I'll come by. There's nothing I'd like more than to get drunk with you."

Jimmy is a real Baja pioneer. His book, *The Grinning Gargoyle Spills the Beans*, is a hoot. It's about his 45 years of adventures in Baja, and if I'm an ol' (menopausal) broad, then he's a crusty ol' fart—with a heart of gold. He did come by to see me the next afternoon, we did have a couple of drinks and we did yack up a storm. If you're ever in Los Barriles, ask where to find him at Tío Leo's or Mañanas restaurants. He will entertain you for hours. Guaranteed.

We cruised over to Todos Santos on the Pacific coast. We had lunch there with our friends Janet Howey and Howard Eckman. Janet runs the best bookstore in all of Baja Sur, called Tecolote Libros and Howard publishes *El Calendario de Todos Santos*—the guide to everything that's happening in town. We love Todos Santos, and hadn't been there in almost two years, so this was for us, a very quick fix. Once the kids are in college, it's at the top of our list of places we want to experience intimately. We figure it will take us months and months to achieve that goal—and who knows—maybe we'll end up building a house there. It has everything we lust after: it's an oasis, with palm, mango and papaya groves set against the backdrop of La Sierra de la Laguna Mountains, big beaches that go on forever with hardly anyone on them, and a community of artists, writers, musicians and other free thinkers. It's a place that somehow, almost bridges the gap between heaven and earth, and inspires creativity on all levels—a magical place like Sedona, Santa Fe, Taos and San Miguel de Allende. It's definitely a second world experience.

Over lunch, in the sultry, lush patio of the Caffé Todos Santos, Janet asked me if I knew where Chuck Potter was. She'd just reopened after the summer, and he was overdue to deliver her fall shipment of books. Now, we knew where Chuck was. He's the major book distributor for Baja Sur, and he happened to be hanging out a few miles south of us at the Spa—at his house in La Ribera. Somehow (magically?) he showed up in front of the bookstore in his noisy diesel camper, with his little dog Chile riding shotgun, just as we were leaving.

Waving goodbye, we headed south to Cabo, across about a dozen sections of washed out road with minor detours left over from Juliette's visit. Even still, it only took us an hour to get there. Chuy had a surprise for us—a complementary room at the Sol Mar, right on the beach at the southernmost end of the peninsula—on the Pacific side. Here we were able to watch the sunset, before heading off for dinner at The Office—a restaurant right on the sand where you can get your toes wet while dining if the tide's high enough. It wasn't that night, but we did get to see the nearly-full moon rise up over the Gulf while munching one of the most delicious, authentic Caesar salads around.

Here's a little tidbit of Baja lore. The Caesar salad originated in Tijuana. I swear. At Caesar's Restaurant on Avenida Revolución. As a matter of fact, my mother was able to get their recipe a couple decades ago and it's in my cookbook. It's become a Mexican mainstay, like the Margarita and is now served, not just in elegant restaurants all over Baja and mainland Mexico, but worldwide. White-jacketed waiters continue to slide carts alongside diners' tables and whip these salads together in front of their astonished patrons with great pomp and circumstance. The Caesar salad is an edible art form in Mexico, and one you should go out of your way to try in your travels south of the border.

The next day we went snorkeling at Chileno Bay and had lunch with Mary Bragg, the Tequila Man's wife, at their place—Pancho's Restaurant and Tequila Bar—in Cabo. There, I had yet another Caesar Salad—only this time with grilled chicken on it. Major yum. Then it was back to the East Cape. Quick trip. Way too quick. But great nonetheless.

The Baja Babes

Meet the Baja Babes
Getting Wild and Crazy since the '90s

If you ever thought getting wild and crazy in Mexico was a "guy thing," I hereby plan to prove you wrong. This past fall I had the opportunity to meet a group of 14 women in their 30s and 40s from Oregon in Buena Vista. While in "real life" they have responsible jobs—like police officer, judge, soldier and businesswoman—in Baja they are just the Babes. The Baja Babes. Each one has a Baja nickname, bestowed on one of their trips. Check them out:

Beth is "La Capitán" in mixed company, and "Captain Spanky" among the Babes. Apparently, there was a spanking incident a few years back when they were having a naked snorkeling adventure on a secluded beach not far from the Spa.

Lacey is "Big Wettie Wet Spot" because there's always a wet spot near or on her body due to drink spillage.

Leslie is "Barbie" because she spends way too long primping and hogs the bathroom.

Lenora is "La Whora" because it rhymes and it makes them laugh.

Linda is "Spook." She got this name one year when she adopted a stray cat that was hanging around resort. One afternoon, as she was holding him, he saw a dog on the patio and totally freaked out. She was wearing a white gauze blouse and the cat tore it to shreds in his efforts to escape. There was blood on it too—giving her the look of a pirate. But that wasn't what earned Linda the nickname. What did was the terrified look on her face.

Lynn is "Princess" but would rather be treated like a queen.

Lori is "Winky For-For-For." Okay. The Winky was apparently coined during the nude snorkeling event. Aside from the spanking, there appeared to be some winking going on too. I don't know about you, but I can visualize all those naked white butts floating topside while the Babes were checking out the fish below. The "For-For-For" was earned when she tried to say, "por favor" and couldn't quite pull it off.

On a tamer note, Patty is "Spidey" because she reminds the others of a spider.

Tami is "Hair gone Verde," because her hair turned green in the pool one year. She introduced herself to me as simply, "Verde." Her long fingernails were painted aquamarine for the trip to match the name.

Maggie is "The Little Mermaid" because she learned to swim in the Spa pool a few years back.

Loraine is "Judge Lips" because it's her fantasy to open a court session one day with a certain rude gesture, accompanied by the words, "Read my lips!"

Rishell has two handles. One is "Jacques the Puffer Fish Catcher." The other is "Medicine Woman." Rumor has it, she plays a doctor on TV.

Rhonda has two handles too. She's the "Village Keeper" because she builds a miniature village on the beach at the Spa every year from bits of driftwood and other flotsam and jetsam she finds. Her other name, "Captain Ron," was earned because she skippers the shuttle on their houseboat trips up north.

Suzanna isn't a real Baja Babe. She's more an honorary one—at least that's what she claims. Her nickname is "Mama Muke," because she is, after all the official "Mama" for this group of self-pro-claimed "Mukes." What this means I can only guess.

The Baja Babes have been coming to Buena Vista since the early '90s. When they hit the Spa, I can vouch for the fact that they pretty much dominate the scene at the swim up bar. They remind me of the raucous, hard-partying fishermen from earlier days—but they're women, of course. They're fun. Run into them down there sometime, and I guarantee you that you will laugh until your cheeks hurt and your sides ache.

Here are a couple of their stories:

According to Rhonda, the Village Keeper, "There was that year Loraine couldn't come, so we brought along a blow-up doll to fill in for her. We named her Loraine, and of course she got the red light in the airport and had to be searched. Blow-up Loraine did naked synchronized swimming in the hot tub with Verde, Little Mermaid, Captain Spanky and La Whora one night. Another time, she hooked up with two Greeks in a stretch limo.

"Then there was the time the other Babes broke into my suitcase, autographed my underwear and paraded them around the swim up bar. I never leave my luggage unlocked anymore."

The Babes go on four-wheeling expeditions down the beach in the convertible Bugs. "The times we've gotten stuck, we just pile out, pick up the Bug and move it to harder ground," explains Rhonda. "Even trips to the airport going home are fun. I remember one year we all loaded up our stuff to drop at the airport. We planned to run into San Jose del Cabo for lunch at Tequila's. However, the only gas station on the way to the airport was closed. Both Bugs were on empty. We decided to make a run for it. If one car ran out of gas, the other would keep going as far as it could. The survivors would then walk to the nearest gas station, get beer and gas and come back for the others.

"Believe it or not, both Bugs made it all the way on fumes." They got their lunch and they got to drink it with cold beer.

My Mexican Dentist and I

Reflections on my Mexican Dentist
Winter, 2002

Just about every American I know who lives in Mexico swears by their Mexican dentist and their Mexican vet. Many weekenders do too. Just the other day, my friend Doris (who's in her early 80s) called me. She was confused about the new Mexican area codes, which took effect in November. She needed some dental work done and wanted to call to make an appointment. How was she supposed to dial, anyway?

"Just insert a 46 after the first 6," I told her. "You'll get right through." Doris drove down to La Bufadora and spent about a week, going back and forth to the dentist and hanging out at her house overlooking Bahía Papalote.

I have a Mexican dentist too. She's not the same one used by most of our La Bufadora neighbors, but Terry turned me onto her. He's been going to her for seven or eight years. His brother, Homey, came out here for a couple of months from Hawaii last summer so he could get false teeth. His bill for all the extractions and a full set of dentures was only $1,500. They were perfect too. Homey was able to smile for the first time in decades.

So why do we prefer our Mexican dentists? Aren't we afraid we'll be treated in less than sanitary conditions with outdated procedures? Our Mexican dentists, physicians and veterinarians are all exceptionally well trained. How many of us remember when our U.S. medical schools were overcrowded in the '70s and many of today's prominent physicians got their degrees in Guadalajara? I know of quite a few. There are a couple of major differences between Mexican and American doctors. The most obvious difference is cost. I had a tooth extracted this summer for $68. My bill for an implant and complete restoration will be $1,500. The last time I had a crown in the States, my bill was almost that high. And I don't have dental insurance. My vet bills in Mexico have been less than a third of what I'd be charged up here. The second, even more important reason I swear by Mexican medical professionals is their attitude. Let me explain....

I had a crown fall out a while ago. I'd put off going back to Dr. Marina Ramirez since she and her assistant pulled my tooth out six months before. I'm not the world's greatest dental patient to begin with, and the tooth they had to pull was a 30-year-old root canal that had cracked down the middle. Getting it out did not even qualify as "pulling." To put it more accurately, it was pried out of me, using what felt like a hammer and chisel, with way too many loud cracks and crunches for my taste. I was shook up for days afterward and hadn't gone back since. But my crown fell out, so I was forced to go. I called to make an appointment.

"Anita!" she cried when I identified myself on the phone. "How are you? How is my Terry? You need to come this week? I can see you on Friday."

I explained that we were driving down on Thursday. It was a 45-minute drive from La Bufadora to her office. "Is there any way you can see me Thursday?" I asked. "It would be much more convenient."

She checked her appointment book. "I have a lady here for 10:00 on Thursday. She's always late. I'll move her to Friday if I can. Call me at 9:00 Thursday and confirm, okay?" Then she asked to speak to Terry to see how his brother was doing with those new teeth.

I tried to call at 9:00 a.m. but discovered that my Mexican cell phone was out of money. I couldn't call. We were early, so we stopped at the Baja Cellular office (which had suddenly been transformed into Telefónica MoviStar) and put pesos on the phone. Then we drove to Dr. Marina's office. It was 9:45. She hadn't arrived yet. When she walked in two minutes later, she apologized profusely for being late. I laughed. "Hey, I'm early!" I told her and explained about the phone. No problem. The other patient had been shifted to Friday and I was ushered to the chair.

We talked for half an hour before she went to work on me. She chatted about her daughter, her mom and filled me in on all the latest happenings in their lives. She told me it was a shame that I wouldn't be able to be in town two weeks from then, because she wanted to take me to a huge women-only fiesta to celebrate the upcoming Carnaval—which is what Mardi Gras is called in Mexico. I knew it was a big deal in Ensenada; I'd attended two years prior. "You wouldn't believe the dresses the ladies wear," Marina told me. "You could come casual like you are now, or you can wear a dress that costs thousands of dollars. It doesn't matter. The ladies, we sit at big tables and drink tequila and champagne. Some of us even smoke cigars—but don't tell Terry I told you that. He might think badly of me!" I assured her that he'd love it.

She went on. "Mexican ladies ... when the men are in the bars or at their own functions ... we get together at private homes. And we are not nearly as boring and ladylike as you might think!"

She's part of a group of about 20 women, varying in age from their late 20s to their 60s. They meet every few weeks and hang out. She told me that anytime I'm going to be around for a while, all I have to do was let her know and she'll invite me to one of the functions. I can't wait....

We'd chatted a bit on my previous visits, but never like this. Marina has lived in the States, and was in fact married to an American previously. She clearly understands the difference between American and Mexican doctors. "When I would take my baby to the doctor in San Diego," she said, "I didn't know him. We weren't friends. It was just in and out as quickly as possible. Here it is different. We Mexican doctors want to know our patients. We want you to be comfortable and know that we will take good care of you."

She did too. She was able to drill my tooth that day without Novocain. She was so gentle that the moment I felt any discomfort (and it was only minor), she stopped, chatted a while and then went back to her drilling. She was able to save the crown. I know my former American dentist would have insisted I get a new one, because it's happened before. The crown is now back in my mouth. I'm over the trauma of the tooth extraction. I may be $68 poorer, but for sure I am one new friend richer.

Before I left, Marina reminded me to have Terry call her and get the rest of his dental work done. "We want him to have his teeth perfect so he can have fresh kisses for you," was how she put it to me. I knew we'd be back. Little did we know it would be three weeks later, when I bit into a taco and came away with a piece of tooth. Actually, that trip four out of five of our group visited Doctor Marina, and a couple other friends snagged her cards from us. It's a trend....

Fun in the sun on the beach in Rosarito
Photo courtesy of Laura Wong, *Baja Tourist Guide*

PLACES....

Grab Those Fun Tickets and Head to Rosarito Beach!

I frequently get asked what there is to do in Rosarito Beach. Wow ... is that ever a loaded question. Rosarito describes itself as having something to fit every lifestyle and every wallet. That means there are plenty of good times to be had; no matter how many fun tickets (money, in case you don't know) you have in your wallet to spend. If you like shopping, dining, nightlife, riding horses or ATVs up and down the beach—Rosarito's got it all. If being pampered in a luxurious spa is what you're craving—you can get that here too. How about just kicking back at the pool or on the beach sipping a cold drink? Rosarito's beach is wide, white and endless. Hankering to dance oceanfront—to rock n' roll music? There are wild and crazy bars like Papas and Beer where you can ride a mechanical bull, shoot tequila and party 'til the roosters crow. There are sedate and elegant restaurants and nightclubs too, and plenty of places in between. The famed Rosarito Beach Hotel—hangout of the rich and famous during Prohibition—hosts an authentic Mexican buffet and floorshow on weekends. There are probably more options for tourists here than anywhere else on the Baja peninsula. Except Cabo.... Rosarito is about having fun ... period. It hustles and a bustles like a big city, but underneath it's as laid back as any resort. The city itself isn't all that large, although it encompasses over 20 miles of coastline. In town, there are only a few traffic signals. Yet there's always traffic on the road and people on the sidewalks—no matter what time of day or night you venture out. This town is flamboyant—and proud of it. Where else can you find a hotel that looks like an amusement park— with a vibrantly colored roller coaster weaving up and down its facade?

Rosarito is a bright and lively place-bursting at the seams with life. You can stop in, spend the afternoon ... the night ... the weekend. Pick a hotel, either in town or on the beach or bluffs to the north or south. Stash your bags, park your car and hit the streets. That's what Terry and I do when we're there.

Rosarito is a shopper's paradise. Trust me. This is the best place in Baja to look for hand-made Mexican furniture; and I am slowly but surely furnishing my La Buf house from here. There's also pottery, wrought iron and folk art. Not too long ago, I was in the market for a four-foot round dining room table—one that could withstand some serious living. Our Boof house didn't have electricity at the time, so we needed a table with a tough enough finish to withstand candle wax and teenagers. I dragged a very reluctant, whiny Terry up and down the main drag for two hours. (I don't get it. He can watch sports all day ... but shopping? He burns out in 15 minutes.) We stopped in every single furniture store. We didn't find what we were looking for and we didn't want to wait 10 days to have a table custom-made for us, so we kept looking. After about a dozen shops (where I wanted to buy everything in sight), I found "the" table at a phenomenal store called Apisa. The table had a "Sold" tag on it, but that didn't matter. There was another just like it in a truck out back. Two guys dug it out for us, cleaned it off, loaded it into our van and we were off.

Anyone who's looking to furnish a house Baja-style won't be disappointed in Rosarito. Even if you're looking for the finishing touch for a room, a unique object d'art, or the perfect gift—you'll find it in one of the shops or arcades here. If you're a man and you hate shopping as much as Terry does, then drop yourself off at Rene's Sports Bar right by the tollgate and hang out while your lady shops herself silly.

Rosarito is also a food-lover's paradise. There are taco stands on every corner, plus a huge assortment of restaurants tailored to fit every budget and delight every palate. You can dine at Calafia down the road, a restaurant terraced down a cliff overlooking the waves, or poolside at Las Rocas, with a stunning ocean view. The best lobster on the west coast is in Puerto Nuevo, a few minutes south.

Once you've had dinner, if you're a night owl (or a college student), you can party just as hearty as if was 1999 (like the song says) at any number of bars. When you're good and tired, head back to your hotel room, pull the blinds, crawl into bed and sleep 'til noon.

Throughout the year, Rosarito hosts a wide range of special events. There's a lobster festival, volleyball tournaments, one of the biggest bike races in North America and lots of other sports, musical, cultural, art and gourmet-dining events going on all the time. The annual fair in July is an adventure and a half. Year-round you can visit Foxploration at Fox Studios, where the blockbuster movie *Titanic* was filmed, and gain unforgettable insight into behind-the-scenes secrets of movie making.

By now you've probably figured that there are too many good times to be had in Rosarito not to stay for at least a weekend. But, for San Diegans like me—it's so close to the border (only 18 miles) that we can drop in for an afternoon of shopping, drinks and *antojitos*—snacks—and be home in time for dinner.

* * * *

Postscript:

Just south of the Rosarito Toll Booth, on the free road heading out of town, is a funky hotel called Baja del Sol on the right side of the road. It's where we stay. It's cheap, we can sit on the balcony in front of room, put our feet up on the wall and watch the waves break. Plus, it's close to town—without being in the thick of things. Adjacent to it is one of the coolest bars in northern Baja. The drinks are great, there's dancing on weekends 'til the wee hours and the bartender, Luis, is known by all the expatriates in town as the "Dean Martin of Baja." There is definitely a resemblance. Tell him Ann and Terry sent you when you stop in. Maybe he'll even burn you a CD of the Philharmonic Orchestra playing Mariachi music—with a Mexican conductor of course.

The whimsical herd of Holsteins in front of Galería Giorgio Santini.
Photo courtesy of Henriette Goldsmith

Northern Baja—An Emerging Art Mecca

To most tourists, when they hear the word "art" in reference to Baja, what comes to mind are the masses of curio shops you see on Avenida Revolución in Tijuana. You know, those little stalls filled with colorful blankets, piñatas, clay pots, silver jewelry, leather goods and other touristy trinkets.

There's more, however. Much more. In the last few years there has been a virtual explosion of galleries offering serious art in northern Baja (and in Baja Sur as well). The artists were always there; they just lacked the money for canvas, paint and other supplies. They also lacked places to display and sell their work, not to mention encouragement and support from gallery owners who believed in them so that they could develop their talent.

Let me take you on a quick tour of my three favorite art galleries in northern Baja. The first is the Giorgio Santini Gallery of Fine Art, located south of Rosarito and just north of the lobster town of Puerto Nuevo on the free road. The second is the Galería del Mar in the Arcade at the Rosarito Beach Hotel. The third is the Galería Berta Armas in Punta Banda, southwest of Ensenada on the road to La Bufadora. Stop in and visit one, two or all three of these galleries the next time you're in Baja. You will be amazed and impressed, I promise you. You'll also be delighted. You might even find a remarkable piece of art that you absolutely cannot live without. And ... you will definitely be back for more!

GIORGIO SANTINI GALLERY OF FINE ART

In May 1999, Aldo Giorgio Santini opened the Galería Giorgio Santini. He renovated an existing house and created seven showrooms on four levels. It's hard to miss, even from the toll road, because there's a herd of whimsical Holsteins made out of washing machines out front. There are three patios and a caffé, where visitors can sip espresso, tea or wine and eat gourmet snacks while listening to strains of classical music. Galería Santini is the largest privately owned gallery in Baja California and showcases the work of the best artists from all over the peninsula. The atmosphere is unlike anywhere else in Baja. Situated right next to the Pacific, with mountains rising behind it to the east, it's a peaceful and relaxing location. The facilities are spacious, elegantly designed and inviting.

Aldo Santini is my age and very cool. He was born in Rosarito. His family has owned this piece of land since 1952. His mother was Mexican and his father, Italian, so, although he was born in Mexico, he was raised in Italy and the Canary Islands. He opened his first art gallery in Milano, Italy in the late '70s with his cousin. After four years, he moved back to Mexico and spent several years practicing his profession of architecture until 1993, when he moved to San Miguel de Allende. There he opened his second art gallery, Galería del Pueblo, which is still going strong. In 1999 he returned to his roots in northern Baja, committed to creating a place where renowned local artists could display their paintings, sculpture, mixed media and glass art in an appropriately aesthetic setting.

"Painters who don't sell their work stop painting. They can't afford to buy more paint, because it's expensive," Aldo told me. "However, if their work is promoted, they sell, they paint more and they improve. This is a labor of love for me. I want to help them. We have the best artists in Baja norte here and we offer them a dignified space."

Most artists featured here are Mexican, but Galería Santini exhibits paintings by Americans, Europeans and Latin Americans who live in and around Rosarito as well. Giorgio envisions his "Rancho

Santini" growing into an artist colony, similar to Todos Santos in Baja Sur. He plans to add a foundry so people can sculpt in bronze and also to add studios and offer classes—so that little by little, it will become a haven for the art community.

Just 600 yards to the south is Santini's second Baja gallery, Rincón de Arte, which offers more art and fine Mexican handcrafts. There are no curios here—only authentic pieces created by talented artisans from all over the country. In 2001, Santini opened a third gallery in the lobby of Fox/JVC Presents, the brand-new theater at Foxploration, Fox Studios Baja's behind-the-scenes movie park. Collaborating with him on this project is Berta Armas from Punta Banda.

Galería Santini is a magical place, and Aldo, his wife Angelica and son Giorgio are the most gracious and friendly of hosts. The art there is intense, alternately primitive and sophisticated with touches of surrealism here and there. There is passion, great beauty and a commitment to enabling the art community in Baja to unfold like the wings of a butterfly.

GALERÍA DEL MAR AT THE ROSARITO BEACH HOTEL

Armando Gonzalez is a big, handsome bear of a man who's married to a writer friend of mine, Paula McDonald. He's also the owner of Galería Del Mar, and known for being one of the most astute and discerning art dealers in Baja California. Since 1983, when he opened the contemporary art gallery, Contrapunto on Prospect Avenue in the heart of La Jolla, California and then later moved back to Tijuana to open Galería Dimensiones in Tijuana's Río area, he has continually sought out talented, undiscovered artists and then worked hard to develop and promote them. He has a knack for spotting exceptional ability at an early stage. During his five years in the Río district, he presented 60 individual and collective exhibitions of top artists, both local and global—many of whom are now highly celebrated artists throughout Mexico. These include Blancarte, Valra, Lameiras, Pereznieto, Galindo, Moret, Mendez Calvillo and Pal Kepenyes.

In 1987 Armando opened Galería Del Mar in Rosarito. Since then he has consistently presented a dynamic combination of established artists and those he believes to be the stars of the future. He displays the work of Jorge Imana, currently celebrating more than 50 years as a painter, Silvia Galindo, with more than 40 individual and collective shows to her credit, Francisco Merino, a long-time favorite, the French story teller/painter, Daniela Gallois, the conceptual works of Rosarito-born Ron Glaubitz, the extraordinary and often mystical works of Hugo Crosthwaite, considered one of the most skillful and dramatic artists on the west coast today, plus the miniature etchings of Guadalupe and Enrica and the batiks of Raquel Roldan.

For several years, Armando has a been a curator of the prestigious Galería La Esquina De Bodegas at the Santo Tomas Winery in downtown Ensenada and at Centro Cultural Tijuana, Tijuana's main cultural center, with four major exhibitions.

Galería del Mar reflects Armando's personality. With its friendly, casual and eclectic atmosphere, it invites the art lover to explore and discover that very special work of art that will truly enhance a personal collection. He will delight you with his wit, charm, knowledge of art, Mexican culture, customs and history, world film, gourmet food, fine wines, world travel, world politics and more.

GALERÍA BERTA ARMAS

On the eastern outskirts of Cantú, en route to La Bufadora, you'll find the Galería Berta Armas. You can't miss the blue and white building on the left hand side of the road. There's a large abstract painting across the top and two paintings between the arched windows. Stop in for a serious look around. You won't be disappointed. Owners Berta Armas and her husband Rich Wallstrom are super friendly, informative and enthusiastic, and Berta is gifted artist herself. Born in Chile, she's been exposed to art her entire life. After traveling extensively in Europe and South America, she studied at the Laguna Beach College of Art and participated in the Laguna Beach Art Festival. Before coming to Mexico, she returned to Chile and studied at the Beaux Art Academy.

The couple opened their gallery in 1994 as a community collective, with the goal of breathing some life into the Ensenada art community. "Since then," Berta says, "We have all grown together. My relationship with my artists is a very close one. I do a lot of pro bono work. I give them supplies, stretch their canvasses and provide encouragement. I represent what I consider the most unique of Baja—new and established talent." She goes on to explain, "My criteria for selecting the art is very personal. It must be contemporary, but, most importantly, I must see and find the artist in the work."

Galería Berta Armas displays sophisticated, often high-end art and sculpture that tends to be expressionistic—avoiding perfect landscapes and still lifes. Each piece reflects the personal vision of the artist, his or her unique perspective. Armas promotes a non-classical use of color and often quirky compositions. "In other words," she surmises, "the work will surprise you. More often than not, it will make you think, feel and see things from a different point of view." Among the artists represented here are Estela Hussong, José Hugo Sanchez, Francisco Merino Carlos de Latorre, Josefina Pedrín, Lucille de Hoyos, Ricardo Corral and Mati Ransenberg.

As I said before, Berta has been co-curator with Armando Gonzalez for six years for the Gallery La Esquina in Ensenada. She is also collaborating with her friend, Aldo Santini on the new gallery in Foxploration at Fox Studios Baja.

Foxploration: Canal Street and its
Hello Dolly Fountain, courtesy of Fox Studios Baja

The Magic of Movie Making ... South of the Border
Since 1996

Remember James Cameron's *Titanic*? Did you know that almost all of it was filmed in Baja, just below Rosarito? Well ... it was.

Back in 1996 and early '97, every time my kids and I made the trip south to La Bufadora, we rubber-necked like your typical, gawking tourists whenever we drove by the brand-new Fox Studios Baja. We were curious to see what was going on with the enormous, nearly life-sized ocean liner that floated there in the world's largest saltwater tank. We watched the ship being built. We watched it "sail." We watched it sink—and it didn't go down fast, like it did in real life or appeared to in the movie. Actually, it took several weeks to film Titanic's descent into the deep.

I'll never forget driving south on the toll road one night in January of 1997. I was by myself, with Snugs as my traveling companion. The sky was pitch black. The full moon had just risen up over the mountains. From almost a mile away, I could see floodlights. *Titanic*, listing at more than a 45-degree angle, loomed up in front of me—

solitary, stark and hanging there, suspended in its death throes out there in the darkness. My kids saw it too on our next trip down. Later, when I watched the movie on the big screen, one of my favorite scenes was when Rose and Jack stood together on the ship's bow, as the aftermath of a spectacular sunset colored the sky in varying shades of magenta. We were supposed to believe they were in the north Atlantic. But I knew better. "Sunset over Rosarito Beach," is always my comment whenever I see that shot.

You can bet it caused quite a stir in northern Baja when Hollywood came to town. In addition to regular star sightings and plenty of new jobs for the locals, Fox Studios' arrival gave the resort town an extra boost of sexiness. It isn't widely known that *Titanic* was filmed here. Hardly anyone knows that parts of six other movies (thus far) have been made in Baja as well … movies like *Deep Blue Sea, Weight of Water, Tomorrow Never Dies* and *Pearl Harbor.* With the studio's unobstructed ocean views and combined tank volume (in four tanks) of over 20 million gallons, its modern filtration plant with the capability of delivering 9,000 gallons of filtered seawater per minute, Fox Studios Baja is the premier facility for water related film work in the world today. No kidding. And it's only 20 minutes south of the border.

In May 2001 Fox Studios Baja opened Foxploration, its behind-the-scenes, movie-making park. This isn't a kiddy theme park, although kids will undoubtedly enjoy it. As its creator, Charlie Arneson, explained to me, Foxploration was conceived with a more sophisticated idea in mind—to offer the public an opportunity to go behind the scenes at a real working movie studio, and to learn first-hand about the production process in an entertaining and interactive way. I had the great fun and good fortune to learn about the place up close and personal in the summer of 2000, when Charlie hired me to write the copy for their website. I was a kid in a candy store.

Imagine yourself turning right off the free road and entering Fox Studios Baja, a 40-acre complex overlooking the Pacific—with more than 2,000 feet of oceanfront property. When you walk into Foxploration, you begin with a stroll down Canal Street, New York, an actual movie set depicting a typical lower Manhattan street. Behind the set is Cinemágico, which houses a variety of interactive exhibits, and gives you a chance to experience hands-on movie making. Exhibits include special visual and sound effects, model making, set construction, art design, editing, animation, cameras, lenses, lighting techniques and makeup.

There's a huge *Titanic* exhibit called Titanic Expo. Actual props, sets and costumes from the blockbuster film are on display. You can take a guided tour, learning the history of the ship and the making of the movie. Other interactive exhibits and movie footage from deep submersible dives reveal the *Titanic,* as it exists today on the sea floor.

Fox/JVC Presents is a state-of-the-art video screening room that allows you to view behind-the-scenes footage of recent Fox films, new Fox film previews, as well as other "making of" footage from productions filmed at Fox Studios Baja. There is also an art gallery that features different artists every month, showcasing the cream of Baja California art. We've been to one of Aldo Santini's exhibits there. It was awesome. Nearby is Xavier's School for the Gifted, where kids of all ages can have fun with 50,000 specially designed foam balls.

But, in my mind, Dolly Plaza is the centerpiece of Foxploration. Set against the dramatic backdrop of the Pacific, it features the original fountain from Hello Dolly. It's also a "Sets Boneyard" where you can see and touch actual set pieces from well-known Fox films. Right next to the fountain is Las Olas Open-Air Amphitheater, the perfect venue for a concert under the stars.

There's more, including the Props and Wardrobe Bodega that is a working part of Fox Studios Baja and is used by movie production companies that film at the studio. There is food, and shopping too. Because Foxploration is dedicated to promoting the best of Baja, you can expect to find Tecate beer, brewed nearby in the town of the same name and topnotch wines from the nearby Guadalupe Valley.

Rosa María Plascencio and Enrique Murillo
Photo courtesy of David Hopps

Puerto Nuevo—A Lobster Haven with Humble Beginnings Since 1954

In San Diego County, Puerto Nuevo lobster is a household word. Whether or not people have actually visited the place, local restaurants serve up Lobster Puerto Nuevo style every year during lobster season. It's a local tradition, right up there with Cinco de Mayo. The actual town of Puerto Nuevo is just a little south of Rosarito Beach in Baja. My buddy Laura Wong, the editor of the *Baja Tourist Guide* sent me down there to get the scoop on how it all started, and here is that story....

In 1954 Rosa María Plasencia's father came to live in what's now the famous lobster village of Puerto Nuevo. He came because he'd heard there were lobsters there—lots of them. There were. A year later Rosa María's mother's family came. The two young people met, fell in love, married and built a tiny house across the street from what is now the family restaurant, Puerto Nuevo II.

At that time there were only two or three families living on the cliffs overlooking the Pacific. Every day the men went out to sea in their pangas. Every afternoon their wives would scan the waters until they saw their husbands' boats materialize on the horizon. Once a positive sighting was made, they'd rush to heat up beans and rice, pat out some fresh tortillas and put a kettle of lard on the fire. The men always came back ravenous, and when they unloaded their catch of lobsters, they'd slice a few in half, drop them into the bubbling lard and fry them up. There was no refrigeration back then, so the now-famous meal of fresh fried lobster, beans, rice and tortillas came into being purely out of necessity. The sea provided the lobsters. Beans and rice didn't need to be refrigerated, and the tortillas could be made on the spot. Even to this day, Rosa María and her husband, Enrique Murillo eat mayonnaise with their lobster instead of melted butter. Why? Because that's what was served when they were growing up, and they like it. He says it's way better than melted butter (but it has to be real mayo ... not the low fat stuff).

Occasionally some Americans would show up and ask the men to take them fishing in their pangas. When they came back in, they'd join the Mexicans in a big meal. As is typical still today at fish camps up and down Baja, no money changed hands. The principle down here has always been, "barter is better," because everyone makes out. The Americans shared soda, ham sandwiches, cookies, candy and whatever else they had to spare in return for the fine food.

In about 1956, Rosa María's father sent to Guadalajara for his brother and sister. They came and joined in the fishing and cooking. A few more families migrated to the area. One built a little stand next to the bus stop, where the welcoming arches are now. They sold sodas, snacks and burritos. Next to their stand was a billboard advertising Newport cigarettes. The Americans named the village after that sign, which, translated into Spanish, is Puerto Nuevo.

Over the years more and more people came from central Mexico. Some were intent on making their way to the U.S.A., but stayed to fish and serve lobsters to the ever-growing crowds of visitors. A political activist, Señora Renterría, helped the families in Puerto Nuevo to get a grant from the government so they could have additional land to build on. She succeeded in getting 17 plots of land assigned to the locals and in gratitude for this, they named the village's main street after her. Restaurant Puerto Nuevo I, founded by Rosa María's aunt and stepfather, was built on the first lot assigned. Puerto Nuevo II was built on the second lot, and got its name because of it. A third family built yet another restaurant. All of them charged about 50 about 50 cents for a lobster dinner back then. According to Enrique, people didn't just order a dinner apiece. They came in large groups and ordered lobsters by the half or full dozen. They picked the live lobsters out themselves and watched, as they were sliced open and fried in sizzling lard. Even though their husbands have passed on, all three ladies who helped found the first three restaurants are still alive today to witness their thriving village with its current total of 34 restaurants.

A major growth spurt occurred in Puerto Nuevo in the '70s when the Ortega family came to town and built four restaurants, which they publicized widely. The signs for all the Ortega's are easily visible from the toll road and these days, three to four thousand people make the trip to Puerto Nuevo to enjoy lobster dinners each week. Some come after a shopping trip to Rosarito, others on their way to or from Ensenada, some come on their way to or from southern Baja, but most come just for the food. There are several upscale hotels nearby now. There are also plenty of shops, where visitors can buy souvenirs from their visit to Mexico's most famous lobster village.

A couple of years ago, representatives from one of Mexico City's most renowned restaurants, Hacienda de los Morales, came to visit Enrique and Rosa María. This is a restaurant where presidents dine and governors' daughters get married. The owners flew the Murillos to Mexico City and had Rosa María teach their chefs how to prepare lobster, rice, beans and even tortillas Puerto Nuevo style. They convinced her to pass on the secret recipe for her legendary smoked marlin with mushrooms and chipotle (jalapeño chiles, roasted in adobo) sauce. Hacienda de los Morales anticipated selling about 50 lobster dinners a day when they introduced them onto their menu—but at last check they were selling upwards of 80. That would indicate, it seems, that Puerto Nuevo has become famous, not just with locals and American tourists, but on a national level within Mexico. It's a fame that's well deserved and hard earned, just as Puerto Nuevo is a place not to be overlooked by travelers heading down the road to Ensenada.

In case your mouth is watering big time at this point, you might want to mark your calendar. On the second weekend in October, Puerto Nuevo celebrates its annual Wine and Lobster Festival. This lively, not-to-be-missed event takes place on Avenida Renterría, which is shut down to traffic for the day. The best folklórico dancers from Tijuana, Rosarito, Ensenada, Tecate and Mexicali compete to see which city has the most talented dancers. Several Baja wineries offer samples of their top-of-the-line wines. There's a contest to see which restaurant makes the best tortillas, which has the most festive and colorful decorations, and a race where waiters, carrying a tray with three glasses and a bottle of wine run all around the village. Sounds like fun, huh?

Sunset at Monte Xanic

Baja's Exotic Wine Country
Since the 1990s

The *Fiestas de las Vendimias*—Wine Harvest Festival—in and around Ensenada, takes place every summer in August. Because I was writing an article about the festival during the summer of 2000, Terry and I were invited to the kick-off celebration at the Ensenada Cultural Center. We donned our party duds and headed north to sample wines from all the wineries, along with appetizers from Ensenada's finest restaurants. The next night was the Street Fair at the Bodegas de Santo Tomás. We brought Gayle, Chelsea, Derek and Gonzo to this event with us. We were planning to meet Keith, from the Spanish language school. Trouble was, he was on Mexican time and we were on camp time. The kids got bored and as whiny as two-year-olds, so we left by 8:30—which was about five minutes before Keith arrived.

On Monday night we had the premier experience of Teenage Summer Camp—most likely because we took a day off. We left the kids at home under Bucky and Russ' supervision and got a room in Ensenada with a view of the harbor. Our pila had been on empty and we'd been waiting for the water truck for almost two days by the time we left, so a hotel room with a hot shower was a serious treat. However, it was nothing compared to the concert we experienced at the Monte Xanic (pronounced MOHN-tay Shu-neek) Vineyard. It was held just after sunset, right in the vineyard and it was performed by a troop of opera singers with a full orchestra from UABC—the Autonomous University of Baja California. I didn't even know I liked opera until that concert. There were very few Americans among this crowd of about 300 well-dressed Mexicans. The setting was idyllic, outdoors on a hillside behind the winery, overlooking a reservoir, the vineyards and gently rolling hills that faded away as dusk turned to night. It was romantic, balmy, warm and intimate—a perfect evening we wished would never end.

* * * *

The rolling hills and lowlands of the Guadalupe Valley, just northeast of Ensenada, and the Santo Tomás Valley to the southeast are covered in vineyards. The wineries in this area produce nearly 95 percent of Mexico's wines.

The winemakers of the Guadalupe Valley are as passionate about making great wine and as fussy as any Frenchman from Bordeaux. In fact, the conditions here are remarkably similar to those in southwestern France. With ideal marine and atmospheric conditions and porous soil of primarily decomposed granite, these wines rival any produced in California. Grapes thrive in the area's coastal valleys framed by rugged, rocky hills. They are tended to lovingly, picked by hand and fermented with the utmost care, using techniques perfected over the centuries. Give yourself a treat and plan a visit soon. These days they produce an array of memorable wines, including Cabernet Sauvignons, Merlots, Cabernet Francs, Zinfandels, Petit Sirahs, Sauvignon Blancs, Semillons, Chenin Blancs, Fumé Blancs, Blanc de Blancs and Chardonnays.

Winemaking in the Californias actually began in Baja. The Spanish padres planted the first grapes as they worked their way from southern Baja to San Francisco founding missions. The first cuttings arrived at Misión San Francisco Javier near Loreto from Europe in 1699. In 1791 the first vineyards were established at Misión Santo Tomás, in the fertile valley 30 miles southeast of Ensenada. Vineyards were planted at Misión Nuestra Señora de Guadalupe del Norte in Guadalupe Valley around 1934. Bodegas de Santo Tomás, the first official winery, was founded in 1888. It has produced wine consistently since then, and was the only major winery in Mexico until fairly recently.

Tours at the Baja wineries are relaxed, casual, intimate and informative. There are no crowds. You're sure to learn far more about the art of wine making there than at any winery up north—and you'll have more fun too. You'll learn that whites are picked at night and reds very early in the morning—and why. You'll learn about the importance of gravity (in lieu of pumps) in keeping the juice pure as it goes into fermentation. You'll taste the wine right out of the barrels as it's aging.

* * * *

When we visited the Guadalupe Valley, our first stop was the Adobe Guadalupe, a romantic bed and breakfast right in the middle of the valley. It's not easy to find, so it's advisable to get directions ahead of time. We knew what to look for, so we knew when we were close. The stark white of its buildings, accented by red tile roofs, stood out dramatically against the backdrop of rock-strewn brown hills and the brilliant green of the vineyards. Standing alone amidst the vines and marking the entrance to the inn was a water tank with a pair of angel wings hovering over it. Subtly but exquisitely painted in hues native to the valley, it gave me chills.

The Adobe has the spacious elegance of a modern-day Spanish hacienda. We strolled through a courtyard designed by a Persian architect who included 125 arches—so that cool Pacific breezes ricochet around inside, creating a natural kind of air conditioning. Hosts Tru and Don Miller, transplants from Newport Beach, began harvesting their own grapes at their winery in 2001, so visitors can now experience wine making up close and personal.

We hung out with Tru beside her pool one sultry August afternoon and listened to the story of how she came upon this place. "As a Dutch person, I'm usually matter-of-fact and not spiritual. But I was at Notre Dame a few years ago, and happened upon a side altar of the Virgin of Guadalupe. Everyone loves Our Lady of Guadalupe—especially in Mexico. All of a sudden, I got this message: 'You're going to die in Mexico.' I told my husband, and Don said, 'I hope not right away.'

There was a chuckle in my head and the words came: 'Not right away. But you will.'

"I've always been a wine-lover. At the time of this 'visitation' from the virgin, I was the only woman on the wine committee of the Pacific Club in Newport Beach, where we lived. Our sommelier at the club was René Chazottes—the best sommelier in the country and fourth in the world. I told him this story and he urged me to go to Guadalupe Valley. I went. I found this piece of land. It felt right. I called my old Dutch mother and told her about it. She let it be known that she had some cash saved up and wanted to send it to me. Shortly thereafter, I got a manila envelope in the mail. It was $100,000 worth of Dutch gilders—in cash. To the penny, that's what this land cost me."

That one gave me more chills.

In addition to the inn and winery, there's a chapel and shrine dedicated to Our Lady of Guadalupe. It's adorned with Angel's wings and *vaqueros*—Mexican cowboys—tip their hats at the virgin as they ride by. Some leave little gifts, a few pesos and candles behind. People have gotten married here.

After a Mexican breakfast of *huevos rancheros*—ranchero-style eggs—in the morning, we started off to tour the wineries. For the ease of navigation, we backtracked and began from west to east, beginning just south of the third tollgate on the road from Tijuana to Ensenada, where Highway 3, the road east to Tecate, begins.

The first winery we came to was Casa de Piedra, on the left hand side of the road at San Antonio de las Minas. It was established in 1999 by celebrated winemaker, Hugo de Acosta to produce an "author's quality wine." Apparently he succeeded, because the entire 2000 and 2001 harvests sold out—before they were even fermented. Well-known all over Mexico, these wines are a favorite with young professionals in Mexico City.

Practically across the road is Viña de Liceaga, another young winery that produces excellent Merlot, Merlot "Gran Reserva" and Cabernet Franc Blend.

Next stop: Mogor Badan, next door to Liceaga to the east. It has been dubbed a "virtual winery" because all their wines are produced at friends' wineries with grapes purchased in the Guadalupe and Santo Tomás Valleys. It's known for its white Chasselas, red Mogor Badan (Cabernet Sauvignon with different varietals each year).

Heading east again on Highway 3, we ran into the town of

Francisco Zarco, just past a long bridge. Turning left, we drove through. There weren't any signs for the wineries, so it was mandatory to pay attention. The pavement ended and we were on a washboard dirt road. We passed the Russian museum, which depicts the story of the Russian immigrants who settled this valley in 1907. The sign for Monte Xanic popped up, alerting us to turn right. Five wine lovers, whose sole objective was to make world-class wines, founded this winery in 1988. Under guidance of gifted winemaker, Hans Backoff, they have succeeded. They make an array of excellent red and white wines. Our favorite was the Viña Cristel, a mixture of Sauvignon Blanc and Semillon grapes.

Chateau Camous is visible from Monte Xanic, to the west. It was founded in 1995. President of the Ensenada Winegrowers' Association, Fernando Favela, and the winery's Bordeaux-educated winemaker, Victor Torres-Alegre, met us at the front door and gave us a two hour guided tour. Their wines, under the careful supervision of renowned French wine expert, Michel Rolland, have won awards all over the world. Their Gran Vino Tinto, made from a blend of Cabernet Sauvignon, Cabernet Franc and Merlot, has raked in the most honors. Camou also produces a dazzling Merlot, Zinfandel, Fumé Blanc, Chardonnay, Clarete and Blanc de Blanc.

A little further west is Bodegas Valle de Guadalupe, owned by David Bibayoff, who uses a blend of traditional and modern techniques in his wine making.

Back on Highway 3 heading east, the next stop was Casa Pedro Domecq on the left side of the highway. Founded in 1973, this winery is famous throughout Mexico for making both wine and brandy, and is considered the marketing pioneer of Mexican wines.

Last stop on Highway 3 was Vinos L.A. Cetto, just past Domecq on the right side of the road. Founded by Angel Cetto from Italy, this winery offers tastings of wines, coolers, brandy and tequila. We, of course, bought a bottle of wine and had an early dinner—picnicking on the terrace overlooking the vineyards. L.A. Cetto doesn't participate in the Fiestas de las Vendimias, but hosts their own festival in early September with wine tasting, grape stomping, dinner, a bull fight, dance show and fireworks.

The next day, we headed south into Ensenada to visit its wineries.

The first we hit was Cavas Valmar, founded in 1983 by brothers Hector and Gontran Valentín, along with winemaker Fernando Martain.

They produce an excellent Cabernet Sauvignon and Chenin Blanc and their tasting room in Ensenada is located at Avenida Riveroll #1950 at Calle Ambar.

Bodegas de Santo Tomás is the area's oldest winery. Founded in 1888, it has always been known for producing Mexico's basic red and white table wines. In 1992 it launched an ambitious project to upgrade both its vineyards and its winemaking techniques, so it now offers some real world-class wines, including champagne. Their tasting room, restaurants and art galleries are located at Avenida Miramar #666, and are well worth a visit.

Hussongs at Carnaval

Hussongs Cantina—Birthplace of the Margarita
Since April, 1892

Ever been to Hussongs? It's a rite of passage for many
Southern Californians who turn 18 and don't want to wait another three
years before bellying up to a bar. But Hussongs isn't just a bar. It's a
landmark ... a legend ... a one-of-a-kind, not-to-be-missed experience. It
has this certain mystique. It's famous. People all over the world have
heard of it. Its popularity has never waned in all these years. It's also
the place where the Margarita was invented—back in October 1941 by
bartender Don Carlos Orozco. He concocted the perfect mixture of
equal parts tequila, Damiana (Controy is used now) and lime, served
over ice in a salt-rimmed glass for Margarita Henkel, daughter of the
German Ambassador to Mexico. Not too many people know that, and
plenty of other bartenders claimed to have invented the Margarita—but
Ricardo Hussong swore to me that this is the true story.

Hussongs hasn't changed much over the years. Current owner,
Ricardo, is the grandson of founder Juan. He told me that the only
changes he's made to the building since taking it over in 1979 were to
replace the sheet metal ceiling and to add a new ice maker. He's maintained the family tradition of serving consistently great drinks, using

top quality liquor and charging reasonable prices. It's laid back, friendly, casual and always tons of fun. The dark green interior, wooden floors covered in sawdust and funky art on the walls never changes. Mariachis rotate in and out, just like they always have. Whenever a song finishes, there's a round of hooting, hollering and cheering. A guy with a Polaroid cruises by, offering souvenir photos. Another comes in with a pad of paper and charcoal, offering to do your caricature.

Is it rowdy? In a comfortable, easy-going way that doesn't take itself too seriously. It was way wilder in the '70s. Ricardo believes things have calmed down because, as he says (and he's about my age), "We're all growing up. The crowd is mellower now. The younger tourists go to Papas and Beer. It used to be that we had about 85% Americans here. Now most of our customers are locals. Business people come in here for a drink before lunch. Men in their 20s and 30s meet their girlfriends and wives here on Friday nights. It's steady." I know. I've seen it. And on weekends the locals are always happy to share their tables with visiting Americans. At Hussongs, everyone is your friend.

So how did it all start, anyway? Is the name Hussongs really German? And, if so, how did a German end up owning the most popular bar in all of Baja? Well, here's the scoop...

Johann Hussong, the cantina's founder, was born in Germany in 1863. When he was 23, he immigrated to New York, where he became John. After a year, he headed west to California. In 1889 the discovery of gold south of the border lured him to Ensenada. Back then, Ensenada was barely a blip on the radar screen. There were 1,337 people, three hotels, one bar, a pier, a few shops, a flourmill, a school, a stable and a wine cellar. There was a new telegraph and phone line between San Diego and Ensenada and a steamship line that operated between the two cities. The road between the two was pretty much impassible.

John hunted quail, geese and other wild fowl, which he sold to local restaurants. In 1890 he bought a barbershop and began running a carriage with six horses between Ensenada and the gold rush camp, El Alamo, about 60 miles to the southeast on a very bad road. His carriage flipped one day that June, and he broke his leg. He was brought to J.J. Meiggs' cantina in Ensenada to recuperate. A few days later Meiggs attacked his wife with an axe. He was arrested and she took off for California. The day he got out of jail, Meiggs sold the bar to John

Hussong and left to search for his wife. Neither was ever heard of again.

In those days, the cantina was located where Papas & Beer is now. However, the next-door neighbors complained constantly about the noise, so John—who had by then become Juan—moved his bar across Avenida Ruiz, where it's been ever since. In April 1892 Hussongs Cantina was established.

Hussongs has always been a place that piques the imagination and whose memory lingers in the mind. My dad told me about his first visit there. It was 1931. He was nine. His dad and some fishing buddies were inside drinking and told him to wait outside. He couldn't handle the suspense. He had to see what was behind those green doors, so he sneaked in, climbed up onto an empty barstool and ordered himself a Coke. Ricardo told me recently that kids were able to come in and hang with their parents until the early '60s, when the laws changed. That was about the time of my first almost-visit to Hussongs. Like my dad, I was told to wait outside, but I was with my mom and sister so we went next door for tacos. When we finished, we stood out front for a few minutes waiting. I remember the music, the laughter. I remember wanting so badly to be old enough to go inside and see for myself just what all the excitement was about.

I had to wait another ten years ... but I've been coming back ever since. And I finally got to tip one with my dad too, after all this time.

* * * *

Just for fun, here's a recipe for a perfect Baja Margarita, straight from the mouth of Ricardo Hussong:

The Original Hussongs Margarita
1 1/2 ounces tequila
1 1/2 ounces Mexican Controy (Cointreau or Triple Sec can be substituted)
Juice from 2 or 3 limones, or Mexican limes, freshly squeezed (equal to 1 1/2 ounces)
Crushed ice
Margarita salt (optional)

Place tequila, Controy, lime juice in blender. Throw in a handful of crushed ice. Shake well if you want to serve it on the rocks. If you want it blended, then blend until very slushy. Wet rim of Margarita glass with lime and swirl in small dish of salt. Pour Margarita into the glass. ¡Olé!

Carnaval, Ensenada-style

On The Road to Ensenada
Carnaval (Mexico's Mardi Gras) 2000

Chris Isaak really did record his CD, *Baja Sessions* in Baja. He recorded it in Todos Santos, actually. Jimmy Buffett really did spend Halloween in Tijuana and wrote a song called "The Desperation Samba" about his experiences there. I've often wondered, however, whether he knew he was really celebrating *Día de los Muertos*—Day of the Dead—and not Halloween. Another thing I always wondered was whether Lyle Lovett ever really drove *The Road to Ensenada*. I asked this question enough times, and finally, someone in the know told me that he truly did make the trip. In fact, he was spotted near Mike's Sky Ranch east of Ensenada on a dirt road, caked in dust from head to toe and riding a motorcycle. Go, Lyle!

I know one thing for sure. It's easy to tell a bona fide Baja aficionado from someone who's just looking for a catchy title for his or her new CD. Obviously, Lyle and Chris qualify. Jimmy's cool ... no matter what. (I've been a parrot head since the '70s.)

I love the road to Ensenada. I drive it once or twice a month. For seven or so dollars (depending on the peso fluctuation) I have the

pleasure of cruising along the edge of steep bluffs overlooking the
Pacific Ocean and enjoying some of the most beautiful coastline anywhere. I relax. I grin. I literally inhale my surroundings and delight in
everything, from the wide-open spaces where sea, mountains and sky
reign supreme, to the colorful buildings dotting the highway. When I'm
alone, I crank up the tunes and sing at the top of my lungs. Yes, I've
been known to sing along with the above-mentioned artists on these
trips. Never for a moment do I miss the crowded freeways and concrete jungles of Southern California. By the time I reach Ensenada,
about 75 miles south of the border, I am in a totally different head-
space than I was back home.

     Although I love the view coming into town from the north, my
absolute favorite view of Ensenada is coming from the south. Driving
out of La Bufadora, the road winds around the top of the Punta Banda
peninsula and down toward the marshlands of the estero. The grand
bay of Todos Santos appears below steep cliffs, expanding west and
north, a vast and shimmering turquoise-blue body of water surrounded
by the city, a lush fertile valley and crowned, in every direction, by
pale purple mountains. Legend has it that the Spanish padres who first
discovered the bay sat by the fire brainstorming one night, trying to
come up with a name for it. They went through one saint's name after
another, before finally throwing up their hands and just naming it
"Todos Santos," after all the saints. It was simply too big and too
impressive to hang a single saint's name on. I'll go along with that.

     Bahía Todos Santos is home to the bustling seaport of
Ensenada—the busiest port on the west coast of Baja. It has flourish-
ing commercial and sport fishing industries and is an international
shipping center. In the winter and early spring, gray whales and their
calves frolic in the waters offshore. And of course, there is a booming
tourist industry. Tourists mill up and down Avenida Lopez Mateos,
shopping and stopping in at sidewalk cafes to sample local libations.
They munch on street tacos at the world-famous fish market, and of
course they visit Hussongs. If the scene there is too tame, they hit
Papas and Beer, where there's dancing on the tables and waiters turn
people upside down after pouring tequila slammers down their throats.
There are lots of good hotels and plenty of places to eat. You can eat
on the streets with the locals or dine on elegant European and other
international cuisine. There are the after parties for the off-road races,
like the Baja 1,000, the Baja 500, the San Felipe 250 and the Tecate

Alamo 200. There's the Rosarito-Ensenada Bike Race and the Tecate-Ensenada Bike Race. There's a surf festival in the spring, the Hussongs Chili Cook-off in the fall, the wine festival in the summer and the paella festival in the spring. The Newport-Ensenada International Yacht Race, known as the "mother of all regattas" finishes here.

The city's largest and most popular annual event, however, is Carnaval—Ensenada's own version of Mardi Gras—celebrated the six days before Lent every year. In February of 2000, I went for the first time. We got there about 4:00 in the afternoon. Avenida Ruiz was blocked off. There were vendors carrying towers of wildly colored Mylar balloons for sale to the crowds milling through the streets. Every hot dog vendor in the state of Baja California had to be there—and believe me—you haven't lived until you've eaten a bacon-wrapped hot dog off one of these carts. Major yum. Nearly every store had a makeshift counter out front. Revelers could buy drinks and *antojitos*—snacks—just about anywhere, and as long as we had plastic cups or cans, we could walk around with drinks. We even bought some cervezas from a check-cashing establishment, which had been converted into a full-service bar for the fiesta. There was a big midway, there were bandstands on every corner and strolling minstrels in between. Electric guitars competed nonstop with Mariachi bands. People danced to the rhythms of mambo, salsa, ranchero and rock'n roll music.

About nine p.m. the parade started. From our vantage point at a second story restaurant just down the way from Hussongs, we were able to take great photos of the elaborate floats that drove by and to snatch Mardi Gras beads and candies that were tossed our way from the air. We lost Milo. He wasn't at the van at the previously arranged time, so we left without him. He ended up taking a taxi back to La Bufadora for $35 and showed up on our doorstep at midnight, grumbling and fumbling for his car keys. A friend of mine, Connie, told me it's normal to lose at least one person in your party at Carnaval. Two of her friends lost track of their driver too, and had to take a taxi back to San Miguel at five a.m.

Sunrise in Todos Santos

I've Got Todos Santos on my Mind
February 1998

Todos Santos may just be the hippest spot on the entire peninsula. Tourists from nearby Los Cabos flock to Baja Sur's most acclaimed artist colony every day. They come in their rental cars to check out the spectacular beaches with their much-talked-about secret surf spots, to eat lunch in one of its quaint but fabulous restaurants, to see the artists and to visit the Hotel California—supposedly the one the Eagles sang about back in the '70s.

Todos Santos, located 45 miles northwest of Cabo San Lucas and 50 miles south of La Paz, on the Pacific coast of Baja was founded in 1724. It crept along as a remote, inaccessible outpost until the late 1800s when its vast aquifer was discovered. Sugarcane farmers rushed in and it became a booming agricultural community overnight. Today, all kinds of tropical fruits and vegetables are grown in and around Todos Santos. Cattle ranching flourishes. It's an oasis—a tropical paradise without a single five star resort—yet. The most expensive rooms in town are found at the Todos Santos Inn, an upscale bed and breakfast that's located in the heart of the historic district, within walking distance of all the galleries, shops and restaurants in town. There are more modest hotels too—more and more all the time.

Highway 19 runs from La Paz to Cabo and passes through

Todos Santos. It was built in 1986—the year everything began to change. Pavement always does that. In the words of Joseph Wood Krutch, author of *The Forgotten Peninsula*, "Baja is a splendid example of how much bad roads can do for a country." Pavement brings people. People bring along with them the accouterments of and desire for ... progress. Progress isn't always better.

About the time the road was paved, a pair of well-known artists from New Mexico, Charles Stewart and Ezio Columbo, moved to town. This duo played an integral part in perpetrating the American and Canadian artist migration to the area. The permanent population of expatriate artsy types comprised of painters, sculptors, poets, musicians, chefs, dancers and writers, currently numbers over 400.

In addition to being an artist, Ezio Columbo is the Executive Chef at Cafe Santa Fe, a much-celebrated Italian restaurant he owns with his wife, Paula. They helped found the Todos Santos Festival of the Arts, which is held during the first week of February.

Why all the artists? I wondered the same thing myself the first time I was there, so I picked up a copy of the *Spirit of Todos Santos,* the local paper. Now called *El Calendario de Todos Santos*, it absolutely oozed culture and creative energy. There were meetings where artists shared their lives and processes, poetry readings, a monthly writer's series, historical house tours, events featuring folkloric dancers and gourmet food prepared by local chefs. There were medicine women offering physical and spiritual healing, concerts, sing-along campfires, meditation and massage. Stores advertised authentic Mexican home furnishings from Guadalajara and San Miguel de Allende.

According to local painter and gallery owner, Michael Cope, "... the light has the same vortex energy as Santa Fe or the Bermuda Triangle. People talk about the muted colors of the desert. But when you've lived in it, and watched what the light creates, you begin to see in Technicolor."

Author Jeanne Córdoba claims it's the air, "which is infinitely lighter than the atmosphere in La Paz and seems to melt in your mouth like a fine Parisian pastry." She also maintains that the ground itself speaks in Todos Santos. And that time takes on an ethereal quality. Native Mexicans claim it's in *el corazón de la gente*—the heart of the people. Others say that the erotic whisper of its tropical breezes attracts those who are "more curious about than afraid of nature's harsh challenges and sensual pleasures."

When I came back for my fourth visit, right after my cook-book was published, it was the first time I got to stay for longer than a few hours. Upon arrival, Kit and I headed straight for the beach. While he fiddled around under the hood of his Land Cruiser, I took off down a deserted expanse of sand. The air and water were both about 80 degrees. Trailing my toes in the surf and hiking my dress up to my knees, I chased the waves. I wandered, I danced, I cried, I chased peli-cans, I sang and finally, I sat down and wrote poetry in the sand. The mountains behind me rose up like pale purple monoliths. The white-tipped turquoise water in front of me rushed out to claim me as its own child. I lost all track of time.

Kit was relieved when I finally showed up. We got back in the car and bumped up the dirt road through the fields of tropical fruits and vegetables and palm groves toward the center of town. We stopped in at Caffé Todos Santos. Its front room houses an espresso/juice bar and a bakery. Each chair and table is a work of art, having been paint-ed in funky, bright colors. The walls are covered with original works of art. Patrons sit inside or out on the sidewalk, or they cruise through the kitchen and eat on the patio. A courtyard from a nineteenth centu-ry hacienda, it's sheltered from the blazing sun by a canopy of lush greenery and flowers. A soft breeze blows through it, making it pleas-ant even on the hottest of days.

After lunch we walked around the corner and visited with Janet at Tecolote Libros. As usual, the store was packed. Then we took a stroll walk around town and made a visit to the mission, which is now a fully functioning Catholic church. Around the corner is the Hotel California. As we walked into the lobby to check in, the Eagles song of the same name was blaring. Contrary to rumor—Don Henley never did own part of this hotel. It's all hoopla. There were no mirrors on the ceilings and no pink Champagne on ice either, but the view was to-die-for. Looking out over the rooftops and treetops toward the ocean, we watched as the sun slipped into the sea. We could see the mission and plaza in the golden light and hear the ringing of the church bells, mingled with the chanting of evening mass.

When you go to Todos Santos, which you must, go sit in the big plaza—the park just off the main drag into town. Wait until it gets dark and the hot dog carts come out. Actually, the signs on the carts read, "*Perritos Calientes*"— which translates to "Warm Puppies" in

English. Kit and I conducted taste tests all up and down Baja and we concurred that the very best warm puppies (and the cheapest too, at five pesos each) were in Todos Santos, at a cart right across from the Hotel California. What's a warm puppy? It's a spicy hot dog, wrapped in bacon and grilled to perfection, served in a fresh bun and slathered with Mexican white sauce, fresh tomatoes, grilled chiles and onions, mustard, catsup. Oh yeah, another of Todos Santos' sensual treats....

Ann with Oscar at his La Paz taco stand

ADVENTURES

Searching for the Best Baja Street Tacos

The minute I cross the border and head south, visions of street tacos start dancing in my head. Street tacos? In case you don't know what street tacos are, I'll let you in on a secret. They are the best! I could eat Mexican street tacos at least every other day. In fact, Terry and I have been on a mission the last few years to ferret out the best street taco stands and eat there as often as possible.

Here's a little fantasy to get your taste buds all revved up.

Okay. Imagine this if you will—you're walking down the street in Rosarito, Ensenada, La Paz, Todos Santos—anywhere south of the border. You smell that distinctive aroma that tells you someone nearby is barbecuing steak. Your olfactories are instantly electrified; your mouth waters and you turn your head to see where the wondrous smell is coming from. Two stores away is an outdoor counter jammed with people sitting on stools, or just standing, hunched over plates of food.

You move in for a closer look. They're scarfing plates full of tacos. The guy behind the counter tosses a few slabs of carne asada onto a grill behind the counter, cooks them, removes the meat to a wooden board and chops it into tiny pieces with a meat cleaver. He reaches to a bowl, grabs some battered up pieces of fish and drops them into a sizzling vat of oil. Yum. Fish tacos! He reaches off to his left, toward this huge hunk of reddish meat on a spit. Another yum. Tacos adobado, made with spicy, marinated pork. This is taco heaven. He flips some corn and flour tortillas on the grill. When they're steaming, he slips a piece of wax paper under each one and puts it on a tiny white paper plate. He heaps grilled carne asada onto three tortillas on one plate. On another, he piles fried fish and splashes some white sauce onto four more tortillas. The third plate is a combo. This one has a carne asada and fish taco, plus a taco adobado. He passes the bulging plates out to the salivating locals in front of him. They know what to do, and start adding the condiments of their choice. The options include cilantro, roasted jalapeños, cheese, onions, tomatoes, several types of salsa, cabbage, huge radishes and sour cream sauce. They pile on the goodies. You see a couple paying their bill—*la cuenta*. They start to get up. Before they're all the way off their stools, you and your companion have slid onto them. You're ready. Order up. And don't forget an ice cold Coke or a cerveza.

So … are your taste buds revved up yet? Mine sure are. Here is a rundown on Terry's and my "Top Five Favorite Street Taco Stands" (so far). I'll tell you their names, but not their exact locations. You're going to have to scout them on your own—it's part of the adventure.

Rosarito: Yacqui Tacos. Paula McDonald turned us on to this place. They sell *perrones*, which are burrito-sized tacos for about a buck. They're made with carne asada, barbecued cowboy style and served in a big flour tortilla with *queso Monterey*, or Mexican Jack cheese, guacamole and salsa. The roasted jalapeños here are the best … well, in Rosarito anyway. Roasted right along with the beef until partially charred on the outside and soft on the inside, they're sprinkled with fresh limón and salt. They're not that hot usually. Only about the tenth one will light your mouth on fire.

Ensenada: A couple doors down from Doctor Marina's dental office is a place called Tacos El Norteño. This is Keith Rolle's favorite taco stand. It's a stand too, because it consists of a tiny storefront. You have to eat standing up; there aren't any seats. This is another strictly Carne Asada taco joint. We tried it right before one of my dentist appointments. I wolfed down two tacos—made with meat, salsa and guacamole heaped in a corn tortilla, grabbed a toothpick and raced off to see the dentist. When I bragged to her about the great tacos, she told me, "Oh Ann, I know a much better place. Bigger tacos. Cheaper. Better. Homemade tortillas. But it's a secret. I can't tell you where it is. Sometime you come here and you be very hungry and I will take you there and we will have lunch."

This second Ensenada gem is one we've been going to for years. It's so easy to find that I have to tell you where it is. It's right next door to Hussongs. On the left. Ricardo is the chef and he's a delight. He serves up carne asada, fish, chicken and adobado tacos. The array of condiments there is about the best anywhere in Baja norte— especially if you catch him on a day he's made grilled jalapeños. This is the only taco stand on this list that serves beer.

Maneadero: Just south of the La Bufadora turnoff, on the left hand side is Tacos Poblano. The first time I caught sight of this place, I was with my kids. It was about 1995. We were coming back from a day at the waterslide park, a few miles south of town, and we were hungry. I spotted a mountain of radishes off to my right. There was a crowd out front. I pulled over and parked. We got in line. The carne asada tacos there are to-die-for. And, they always have roasted jalapeños. The last time I was there I ate about nine.

La Paz: Terry and I found Oscar's Taco Stand on the malecón with the kids two nights before Christmas, 1999. We were cruising the malecón and had just seen a Santa Parade and a Parade of Lights in the harbor. Oscar's is a portable street stand that is only open at night. He serves carne asada tacos and has a spread of condiments that even surpasses Ricardo's. We were all impressed. He even let me come inside with him and have our picture taken.

Whale photo courtesy of Keith Jones, www.greywhale.com

Following the Whale Trail
Winter through Spring

Imagine this. You're a 49-foot, 73,000-pound, very pregnant gray whale. You've spent nearly two months swimming from the frigid waters of the Bering Sea toward your calving grounds in San Ignacio Lagoon, halfway down the coast of Baja California on the Pacific side of the peninsula. It's the day before Christmas and you've just passed the city of Ensenada and rounded the tip of Punta Banda. As you come up to the ocean's surface to blow, you hear splashing. Raising your massive head up out of the water, you fix a softball-sized eye on a pair of humans (one of them would be me) paddling along in bright yellow boats. Rumor has it, these creatures call what you're doing spyhopping. Right before your head slams back down into the water, you see the humans pointing and shouting to each other. One takes his paddle and taps at the side of his kayak, obviously trying to communicate with you. Now you're really curious.

You spyhop again and slide across the ocean's surface for a

moment before flipping your flukes at them and diving. Your baby moves in your belly and you can tell your time is near. You've been pregnant for over 12 months and still have about two weeks before you reach your winter home in Baja. You signal to the others in your pod to pick up the pace and swim off.

Like the snowbirds who trek from the cold northern climes of Canada and the U.S. to Baja every year to winter on its warm, abundant beaches, the California gray whales—all 24,000 of them—make an annual 10 to 12,000-mile round trip from their feeding grounds in the Arctic to the protected lagoons of Baja. Some of the most playful and prolific of all cetaceans, their population has rebounded from a scant 500 in 1947 when they were put on the Endangered Species List, to what's assumed to be their original number. So remarkable has been their recovery, that they were removed from protected status in 1994.

What drove the gray whales to the brink of extinction? Humans, of course.... Whalers discovered Laguna San Ignacio and Laguna Ojo de Liebre (also widely known as Scammon's Lagoon) in the mid-1800s. There was a worldwide market for whale products back then. Their blubber was rendered to use as fuel oil. Whalebone and baleen were used for corsets, brushes and the spokes of umbrellas. Even after whale oil was replaced by petroleum and electricity, whale meat was still used as cat food. For nearly 100 years, the gray whales of Baja were slaughtered. The whalers would block off the entrance to the tranquil lagoons where the grays mated, gave birth, nursed and frolicked with their young. Their sanctuaries became killing grounds and the waters of the Baja lagoons turned red with the blood of dying whales. Gray whale moms, like the one we met a while ago, had nasty reputations among the whalers, who called them "Devilfish." These females were fiercely protective of their young. Oftentimes, after her baby had been murdered before her eyes, the mother would charge the whaling boats, injuring and killing their crews.

Here are few more facts about the grays. The females are larger than males, growing to about 50 feet and weighing in at 30 to 35 tons. The males only get to be about 46 feet long and weigh 25 to 30 tons. Toothless, they have filters in their mouths (called baleen) that sieve food from the water. They blow about three to five times in a row, then they flip their flukes (or tail fins) and dive for three to five minutes. They can stay down up to 15 minutes. And they can dive to about 400 feet, although they prefer shallower water.

The babies are about six feet long when they're born and weigh about a ton. They nurse for eight months off their mothers, whose milk contains—by the way—53 percent fat. This rich milk helps them build up enough blubber to make the long journey back north to their feeding grounds, a trek they begin at about two months old. Grays become sexually mature somewhere between five and 11 years old. Their mating rituals, which they carry out in the protected waters of the Baja lagoons, are pretty interesting. Think about it.... These massive cetaceans have no appendages to use to hang onto each other. There's no way they could successfully mate without assistance. Because it takes at least three of them to copulate, an adolescent male comes alongside the female and holds her steady while the mature male mates with her. Good training for the future.

For the first 25 or so years that the whales were protected, scientists studied them from afar. In Laguna San Ignacio, the Mexican fishermen didn't dare go near them for fear that they'd be mistaken for whalers and their pangas (fishing skiffs) would be smashed to smithereens. Francisco Mayoral, a local fisherman now in his late-50s, claims that no one who'd ever gotten near a gray whale lived ... until he had his first whale encounter back in 1972, that is. Francisco was out in his panga with some other fishermen one day, rowing to catch the outgoing tide. A whale swam up to their boat. Francisco rowed like crazy for shore. Only this gray followed him! He and the other men in the boat fell to their knees, made the sign of the cross and started praying like the dead men they thought they were. When nothing happened, Francisco opened his eyes, only to see the whale's nine-foot head with its huge, unblinking eye staring right straight at him. Then it slipped back into the water and started rubbing itself up against the boat. It did this, inexplicably, for nearly an hour. Then it swam away.

The locals were dumfounded. They discussed this phenomenal event among themselves, but the lagoon was so isolated that word didn't leak out to the scientific community for a few more years. It was a crewmember from a whale watching boat out of San Diego, the Salado, who was the first known person to actually touch a gray whale, in 1976.

Over the next five or so years, scientists descended on the area with greater and greater frequency. The playful whales—the ones who loved to be stroked and who put on shows for the humans—began to be called "Friendlies." The word spread and tourists began to show up.

Soon the Mexican government began licensing guides to take boat-loads of curious visitors out onto the lagoons to see the whales up close and personal.

Are the whales really safe? Are they really "friendly?" If the answers to both of those questions are yes—then how and why did they come to forgive the humans for a century of ruthless slaughter? No one really knows the answer to that question, but my good friend, Lynn Mitchell, who leads whale tours, says that things have come around so much that the mothers actually teach their babies to come to the pangas. "The babies love to be petted," she says. "And so many of the older ones love to have their baleen stroked. They all love to play. I've even had my boat picked up and carried on a mama whale's back before. And spun like a toy."

The grays show up in Southern Baja about December or January. The last stragglers take off by late April. Because the Mexican government is very strict about who's allowed near the whales, it's necessary to go on a tour with an authorized guide. There's always a group of government observers that watches all the tourists from shore with their high-powered telescopes to make sure no one hurts the whales or ventures into the off-limits areas of the lagoons.

If you're itching to get close to a gray whale, you've got to go to Baja. You can go whale watching in Todos Santos Bay out of Ensenada aboard a large sportfishing boat, or go for the close encounter in a panga out of Guerrero Negro, San Ignacio or San Carlos on Magdalena Bay. We had a Baja whale adventure, on last day of 1999. But more about that later....

Cave painting
Photo courtesy of Keith Jones, www.greywhale.com

Exploring the Baja Cave Paintings—A Virtual Reality Trip

There were four of us. We left our campsite in San Ignacio at
5:30 a.m. and hooked up with our guide and his son at the mini-mer-
cado. Javier, the father, spoke perfect English. The son, Rodrigo, was
shy and hid behind his father's legs as Terry and I climbed into the
back of the rusted-out old pickup. Our new friends, Marilyn and Tom,
got in front.

Javier headed northwest on Mex 1 for a half hour, then turned
east toward the mountains. A little later, he slowed the truck and
turned right onto a graded, washboard dirt road. We bounced along for
another hour or so, arriving at the village of Rancho San Francisco de
la Sierra just as the sun was inching its way up over the mountains.

The truck ground to a stop. Immediately a dozen dust-colored
dogs rushed us, barking like crazy. A scrawny, leather-faced woman
appeared in the doorway of one of the huts, followed by several children. Three men in cowboy hats sauntered over. Within two minutes a
crowd had gathered. Everyone was talking, laughing and gesturing.
Finally, Javier and a trio of men unloaded sacks of flour and sugar
from the bed of the pickup, along with five cases of Tecate beer and
three cases of Coca Cola. The villagers waved and called their good-

byes as we lurched off.

The road ended a while and Javier parked the pickup. From out of nowhere, two teenage boys leading six fully saddled mules appeared. Chatting non-stop, they adjusted the stirrups for each of us. They tied down our packs and hoisted us up onto crusty leather saddles. We organized ourselves into a line with Javier in the lead and Rodrigo taking up the rear and headed down the arroyo along a steep and narrow, and at times almost nonexistent trail. Javier explained that the two caves that we were going to visit, along with Cueva Ratón had been selected by the Getty Conservation Institute in L.A. for archaeological preservation. We headed west and then climbed up, along the wall of the canyon.

I was lost in the scenery ... the tranquility of the mountains. Before I knew it, we'd reached Cueva de las Flechas. I dismounted, tied up my mule and turned. The sight sucked the breath right out of me. My mouth must've hung to my knees as I stared at a mural that reached to at least five times my height. Three ancient, human-like figures stared down at me. The head and left side of the largest figure, on the left, were reddish in color. His right side was black. The middle figure was all red with a black face or hat and the smallest was pure red. All had their arms raised to the sky. Behind the large figure was an enormous deer. Below him was a figure that looked something like a frog—half red and half black again. There was a smaller deer on the far right.

Javier explained. "The colors black and red represent the spirit. A red spirit is good. A black is bad. Most all spirits have both colors. The ones with arrows in them seem to have the most black. They were more evil. If you will look very carefully, you will see that two of these 'monos,' as the human figures are called, have other inverted figures on their shoulders." He pointed to the one of the left. "This one has a human figure on its left shoulder and a sea turtle on its right. The center mono has a human on its left shoulder and a deer on its right." He gestured. "Notice how this mono is shot through with arrows. It has much black in its spirit. That is how this cave was named. It is called, in English, The Cave of the Arrows. It is not common in the caves of La Sierra de San Francisco to see humans shot with arrows. Usually here it is only the animals that are shown being killed. We can only guess there were more black-spirited people here. More fighting."

I pointed at another gangly-looking figure. "What's that?"
"A frog, perhaps. We are not sure of so many things about these indios. They are a mysterious people. Most of them were killed by disease or by the priests who ran the missions during times of rebellion. Their culture was very primitive and the Catholic padres were not interested in their magic, or their pagan gods. They wanted only to make them Catholics. "And," he said, smiling, "to make them to work in their fields. The ones who are left have lost their identity. They have become one with us here in these mountains."

I ran my finger over the faded replications of deer and what looked to be dogs or rabbits and other animals, trying to imagine what these people had been like and what had compelled them to paint like this. Someone tapped my shoulder.

"Please do not touch the murals," Javier said.

I backed off and walked to the opening of the cave, squinting into the sun. For the second time in less than an hour, I was overwhelmed. Majestic cardón cacti stood sentry over the steep canyon walls. Below them stretched colorful layers of striated rock, dotted here and there with tough desert shrubs. At the bottom of the deep arroyo a grove of date palms stood tall, proud and green against the faded dryness, the fronds rustling in the breeze, and disappearing from sight just below the point where an opening in the rocks occurred. I'd had never seen anything so incredible.

"That's Cueva Pintada," Javier said, pointing across the arroyo. "It looks small from here, but it measures 50 feet across at its opening." He pointed. "Can you see the ramps? The Getty people built them. They run the full width of the cave. There are wooden floors inside too."

The guides hoisted us back onto the mules and led us down the trail along the canyon wall and through the mostly dry riverbed, which was, surprisingly, filled with several small, deep pools of water, nestled between boulders. We began to climb the opposite wall of the arroyo. At the entrance to Cueva Pintada, we stopped again. The view from this side was even better, because I could see everything in greater detail.

Cueva Pintada was wide, as Javier had told me, but it wasn't very deep—only 40 feet or so. Half the cave had a low ceiling. The other half was much higher. Because of the density of the rock and the degree of protection offered by the cave itself, most of the murals were still vibrantly colored and easy to discern. Javier led us to the northern part of the cave. It had a low ceiling and was covered in pictographs. We sat as before and craned our heads back to look. The colors were barely faded at all, but the Indians had painted the ceiling in so many layers it was hard to tell one figure from another in places. We saw birds, rabbits and small deer.

Javier explained. "Other caves are larger inside but do not contain the number of well-preserved paintings as this one. This is the most famous and most visited of all the caves. In this region, there are 20 major caves and many smaller ones. In all of Baja over 100 caves have been discovered. More are discovered all the time. All are at least 1,500 years old."

There was an array of people, some red, some black and some half and half—all with arms raised to the heavens. I could tell the women from the men by the pointed breasts that protruded from their armpits. They danced in front of me, over or under laid with a variety of wildlife—mostly deer with antlers and big-horned sheep. A figure, looking like some kind of monstrous sea mammal, leered down at from the ceiling. I was overcome with the obvious respect and importance these Indians gave to the creatures who shared the mountains and coastal waters with them.

"Who discovered this place?" Terry asked.

"We are not sure. We believe that by the year 1890 that several of the rancheros in the area knew of it. The American, Señor Gardner, the writer of *Perry Mason* TV shows came here by helicopter in 1962 to photograph the caves. The people in the ranchos were very much afraid at first. But he was a good man and generous too."

We picnicked at the edge of the canyon, took photos, hoisted our sore backsides onto the mules and headed back. To another reality.

From under the palapa at Ecomundo on Bahía Concepción

Road Trip: Mulegé
November 1998

In November 1998 my kids went to Florida with their dad for Thanksgiving. Terry and I looked at each other and simultaneously said, "Road trip!"

Deciding where to go wasn't hard. We only had eight days. Mulegé would be just far enough. The weather would be perfect and we had friends there.

I hadn't been to Mulegé since I was eleven. My memories of that trip are a little sketchy, but I do recall that a group from the Audubon Society was staying at our hotel. Roger Tory Peterson was the leader of the group, and he allowed Nina and me to tag along on bird-watching expeditions at sunrise and sunset—along Río Mulegé and through the hillsides. We paid him and his fellow bird-watchers back by putting on a water ballet just for them in the hotel pool. Nina sat on a jumping cholla that trip, and it took Mom over an hour to pluck the nasty thorns from her backside. We flew in a friend's private plane. When we got ready to take off to go home, the plane was so overloaded that the pilot had to abort, turn back, land and lighten the load. When we took off the second time, my mom said it was a real white-knuckler. She was no sissy either. In fact, she flew with some World War II hot shots in her time and was always the most fearless flyer in our family. So when she said we came a hair's breadth away from stalling, and barely cleared the mountain at the end of the runway, I knew she wasn't exaggerating. I'm just glad I was too young to understand the danger.

Mulegé is a sleepy town, nestled in palm groves along the only navigable river in Baja. Six hundred miles south of the border and 89 miles north of Loreto, it marks the entrance to the incomparably beautiful Bahía Concepción. The shores of this bay are lined with small coves—each of which houses yet another campground and where every view seems more spectacular than the last. It's a camper's, boater's, windsurfer's and diver's paradise. There's nothing much better than packing a picnic lunch in a cooler on the back of a kayak and heading out to snorkel or fish in the clear, warm, light turquoise waters of the bay, followed by a dip in a natural hot spring. Aside from Los Arcos at Land's End in Cabo San Lucas, Mulegé and Bahía Concepción are undoubtably the two most-often photographed places in all of Baja. Its desolate beauty—the drama of desert, sea and sky set against a backdrop of rugged and powerful mountains is a visual metaphor that describes the peninsula to perfection.

We loaded up the Vanagon with all our camping gear and headed off from La Bufadora an hour before dawn. It was after dark when we pulled into one of the campgrounds in town, right by the river. We'd shared the driving, but we were fried. It had been a long day and all we wanted was some food and a shower—not necessarily in that order.

We opted for showers first, and then walked along the river to a place we'd heard about called Jungle Jim's. We walked in. It was after nine. There was a lone gringo there, smoking at a table, with a rum and coke in front of him, and a Mexican guy behind the bar. We ordered club sandwiches and Pacificos. The bartender rolled a cot into the middle of the dining room and left. The American came up to us. He handed us a pad of paper.

"I'm getting ready to go to bed here pretty soon. If I'm out before you leave, just help yourselves to the beer. Jot down what you had and we can settle up tomorrow."

That was trusting. "Are you Jungle Jim?" I asked. "We were told by some friends to look him up and tell him 'Hi.'"

He chuckled. "I'm Jungle Jim all right," he said, his eyes twinkling. It turned out that he knew everyone in town, of course. His was, after all, the premier watering hole (with great food) for the expatriate community. He had TV too—and this was the place to go to watch Monday Night Football.

"Do you know Roy and Becky from Econmundo?" I asked. He smiled. "Very well."

"Do you know Mike and Carol from La Bufadora?" Terry asked. He smiled some more. We went on to describe them at length.

"You mean that big ol' fly boy from Alaska—the one Roy taught to fly back in the '60s?"

I didn't know about this connection. "What do you mean?"

He gave me a wicked grin. "Let me tell you a story. About a month or so ago, Mike and Roy were in here one night shootin' the bull with the other locals. Mike was tellin' some guys about how he flew all over Baja in the '70s—doin' fishing charters and such. You know what a storyteller he is. He pretty much had the whole bar spellbound. Tales about landing on a dirt road outside Cabo, back when it was nowhere in particular—just a dusty fishing village with no palm trees and no two-story buildings—at the end of the line. Then he went on about how this place was back then, and how the Pig Roast was more of a huge Mexican luau with a six-course meal of roast pork, turtle steaks, ranch-style beans and rice…."

He paused to light a smoke.

I jumped in. "So what does this have to do with Roy?"

He winked. "*Paciencia, mija*—patience, my daughter." He made himself another rum and coke. "Guess I'm not quite ready to go to bed yet. Well, let me see … in the middle of Mike's story, Roy came over and stood right in front of him—all red-faced and frustrated 'cause he couldn't get a word in edgewise. Finally, he got an opening. 'Did you ever fly at Clover Leaf Aviation in Santa Monica back in 1967?' Mike got a real strange look on his face. 'Yeah,' he said. 'Did you know Roy Mahoff!' ' Yeah. He was my flight instructor. Got me my instrument rating. Last I heard he was flying Leer jets at Morton Aviation. Why?' 'Winnie! It's me! Roy Mahoff!' You should've seen the uproar. Thirty-one years later! 'Course, Mike changed his name. He wasn't Winnie anymore, and that made everything even more confusing. I swear, I never laughed so hard in the last year."

Small world….

He gave us directions to Mike and Carol's palapa, at a place called Playa Naranjo on Bahía Concepción. The next morning we headed out. After a couple of false starts, we found the dirt road leading to Playa Naranjo. As dirt roads go, it was practically a freeway. We followed it for almost a mile, through a veritable forest of cardóns and toward the sea. We spotted Mike's van behind a palapa hut, on the north edge of the bay.

They didn't know we were coming. They didn't have a phone, and the coconut wireless—as the gossipy ham radio network is occasionally called—hadn't leaked the news of our arrival. We parked the Vanagon at the side of their palapa and walked around front. It was entirely open to the ocean, and within steps of the water. They were sitting inside, finishing breakfast. The looks on their faces when we came around the corner were priceless. Mike jumped up. "Whoo Yah!" he hollered. "Look who's here!"

We ended up camping at the end of the row, on the southern tip of the beach. There was a huge palapa there that we rented for $7 a day. Showers (cold) and bathrooms (flushing) were close by. Our palapa was tall enough and large enough to drive the Vanagon into and pop up the top. We rigged up a changing area in the far corner, set up our camp table, stove, coolers and chairs ... and we were ready to hang out.

Mike and Carol couldn't have been better hosts. They took us to the Pig Roast at the Hotel Serenidad. As we'd learned previously from Jungle Jim, going to a Pig Roast at the Serenidad is as much a Baja tradition as visiting Hussongs, and the crowd is always eclectic. The Serenidad has an airstrip; so airborne travelers on their way south frequently fly in and spend the night. To other pilots, it's a destination in and of itself. Mike and Carol introduced us to their favorite restaurants. They showed us a hot springs, right on the beach where we lounged in a natural hot tub under the stars. Of course, they introduced us to their friends—an array of entertaining expatriates.

On Monday, we decided to kayak over to Ecomundo and say "hi" to Roy and Becky. Ecomundo is an ecotourism destination and kayaking resort. It's Roy's brainchild and it's totally self-sustaining. The buildings are made from straw and mud. The electricity is solar. Guests can rent a palapa on the beach with two hammocks in it. Add in some snorkel gear, a kayak and a sandwich from their café, and the day's adventure is made. Also on the grounds was Becky's *Galería*

Serena—Mermaid's Gallery—which featured Baja and nature books along with works of art by people in the area.

It was an easy hour, kayaking from Naranjo to Ecomundo. We pulled our boats up on the shore and ordered a beer before Becky noticed us. After awhile, the wind came up. It was not a light wind. I thought it might be a good idea to leave the kayaks there, catch a ride back to our camp, and then pick them up later. "You can always hitch-hike," Becky said. "Everyone does it around here. It's totally safe."

I looked at Terry imploringly. He laughed. I'd always bragged that I was the better kayaker. I was about to get my comeuppance. We kayaked back. It took almost two hours and my arms felt like they were going to fall off. I whined. I begged him to turn back. He refused. About two-thirds of the way back to camp, a pod of dolphins swam up next to us and entertained us with their dancing leaps for most of the rest of way. It helped take my mind off my discomfort.

"Aren't you glad we didn't turn back?" was all Terry said as we slid into Naranjo, exhausted. I fake-whacked him with my paddle.

* * * *

Postscript:

Jungle Jim passed away shortly after this trip. We'd looked forward to visiting him again, and I'd promised to put his Club Sandwich recipe in the next edition of my cookbook. He was a tenderhearted man who always went out of his way to help others. When we were there for Monday Night Football, one of the ladies who worked in his kitchen became ill. He borrowed a friend's car and took her to the doctor—right then and there—leaving another friend to man the bar. That's the kind of guy he was.

Gayle and Derek whale-watching at Laguna Ojo de Liebre

A Holiday Trip Down and Up Baja
Christmas, 1999

I've flown the length of Baja many times since I was a kid, but never made it any further south than Bahía de los Angeles by car until February of 1998—when I made the trip to Cabo and back for the first time with my friend, Kit. This year, over Christmas Break, I made the trip again, only this time it was in a 28-foot motor home with two adults, two teenagers and a dog. We actually came home with two dogs, after adopting Gonzo in Todos Santos—but that story has already been told.

The road from from Tijuana to Cabo is 1059 miles. If you figure that in American freeway miles, it equates to an easy two-day drive. However, when you drive Mex 1, once you get south of Ensenada, the road's two lanes all the way to San Jose del Cabo. If you take some time to learn the rules of the road, driving Baja isn't really all that tricky. The main thing is to drive cautiously and during daylight. Think 45 miles an hour on an average, especially if you're driving an RV or towing anything. When you see a sign with a cow on it, or one that says *Zona Ganado*, slow down. Keep an eye out for livestock. A *vado* is a wash, which can be full of running water after a rain and *topes* are speed bumps, which force you to slow down when you come to small towns. When a trucker turns on his left blinker, he's telling you it's okay to pass. It doesn't mean he's turning left ... hopefully.

This year we were out to explore Baja Sur, from Guerrero Negro, about halfway down, to Todos Santos. We had to go about 500 miles first, however. After driving half a day, we reached El Rosario, a famous Baja stop along the way. We ate lunch at Mama Espinosa's, a landmark restaurant that serves the best lobster burritos anywhere. Then we turned east as Mex 1 snaked its way up to Baja's Central Desert and the famous boulder fields of Cataviña.

Over 100 species of cacti grow in this desolate, lonely part of Baja, 80 of which grow nowhere else on earth. The majestic cardón are related to the saguaro in Arizona. The difference is that cardóns have multiple trunks. They have strong hardwood skeletons that are used as building material on the ranchos. When it rains, they become fat and succulent. They get as tall as six-story buildings and can weigh up to12 tons. Cirios, or boojum trees, live nowhere else on earth, except here and in Sonora, across the Gulf of California—proof positive that the peninsula was connected to the mainland at one time in the distant geologic past. Cirios look like dancing creatures from another galaxy. They have chunky bases that thin rapidly to one or more gangly branches—long ones that wave about like arms and shorter ones that wiggle on tapered ends, like fingers. On top of their heads grow a crown of yellow flowers that look like pompadours. The stark, alien landscape is also home to ocotillos, chollas and that gnarly old man, the elephant tree. We stopped for a potty break and took photos.

After spending the night in Guerrero Negro, the first stop the next day was San Ignacio—a tiny town in a lush oasis that appears as a mirage in the stark, gray, seemingly endless desert. It's home to (in my opinion) the most majestic mission in all of Baja, rising up out of the palms like a mediaeval castle. Founded by the Jesuits in 1728, the present church was completed by the Dominicans in 1786 and has lava block walls that are four feet thick. Cave painting tours in the nearby mountains leave from here and the whale watching at nearby San Ignacio Lagoon make it a favorite stop off point for Baja history buffs and ecotourists.

After snapping more photos, we proceeded east for our first sighting of the Gulf. Baja was believed to be an island by the first

Spanish explorers. That was an easy mistake to make, because it extends over 2000 miles of coastline—not counting most of the zigs and zags. Off the west coast are the cool waters (55° - 70° Fahrenheit) of the Pacific. This ocean offers lobster, abalone, tuna and halibut—to name only a few varieties of its bounty. The much warmer (usually 75° - 85° Fahrenheit) Gulf of California is a 1,000-mile ocean trench that extends between Baja on the west and the Sierra de la Madre Mountains of mainland Mexico on the east. It's home to at least 850 known species of marine creatures—the richest abundance of undersea life anywhere on the planet. Honest.

After dipping our toes in the slightly chilly sea, we stopped for gas in Santa Rosalía. If you ever get the chance, spend the night at the Hotel Francés and sample as much street food as possible in the evening, like Kit and I did on the previous trip. It is, undoubtedly, the street food capital of Baja. I've never had consistently better bread, tortillas, fresh fruits and vegetables, tacos or perritos calientes from street stands anywhere else.

The French settled Santa Rosalía in the late 1870s, after they received permission from the Mexican government to mine the copper ore found in its nearby mountains. The town's buildings were constructed of wood imported from San Francisco and roofed with galvanized iron from France. The French-owned and managed El Boleo Company not only built the town, mines and refinery, they also put in a pipeline to import water and built a seaport to export the processed ore. Although the mines closed down in 1954, Santa Rosalía is still a bustling community—even though tourists usually just gas up and pass through, en route to somewhere else. Its church, La Iglesia de Santa Bárbara is world-famous. It was designed by Alexandre-Gustave Effeil for the Paris World's Fair and was shipped in pieces to Santa Rosalía around Cape Horn in 1897.

We reached our first camping destination after stopping for lunch in Mulegé. We were headed back to Bahía Concepción—this time to camp on the beach at Playa Punta Arena, on the north edge of the bay and around the corner from Naranjo, where we stayed the last time. We set up camp. We dragged the kayaks off the roof and hit the water. We swam. We snorkeled. We were immediately transported into another world. Later, we sat sipping cervezas and watched the sun go down behind the mountains, turning the turquoise water lapping gently in front of us to turn silver and then a pale shade of lavender. It was a

360-degree sunset—framed by barren purple mountains to the left, the shimmering bay in front of us and red and gold crowned mountains off to the right. The waxing moon greeted us a little later, working its way toward fullness. We spent four days on that beach—and (as always) it wasn't nearly long enough....

From there it was on to La Paz, with a stop in the agricultural city of Constitución where, concerned that our rear duals were balding at a dangerously rapid rate, we bought four new tires for $370. Within an hour they were on and we were on the road again. In La Paz we stayed at an RV park in town so the kids could have hookups (think laptops and computer games) and hot showers. Both evenings we walked to the malecón, La Paz' bay front promenade. We watched a spectacular sunset and moonrise, soaked up the beauty and culture of the city that reminds me a little of Río de Janeiro.

I love La Paz. I've loved it since that first trip, in 1961. Known as *El Puerto de Illusión*—the Port of Illusion, it has a long and color-ful history, complete with Spanish galleons being chased by English pirates and battles being fought in its streets during the Mexican-American War. It's an elegant, sexy, seafront Mexican city that comes alive at night as lovely señoritas in high heels parade down the malecón on the arms of handsome young men. It's tropical, non-touristy, lively and musical—a modern Mexican city set against the backdrop of a glittering bay full of yachts, plummeting pelicans and larger than life sunsets. There's sport fishing and diving off Islas Ceralvo and Espiritú Santo, not to mention visits to a sea lion colony and incredible beach combing and free camping at Playas Tecolote and La Balandra.

Todos Santos was the end of the line for us. We headed for Playa San Pedrito, one of the famous surfer beaches south of town, where we set up camp for another four-day stint. The weather was per-fect—low 80s during the day with more of those 360-degree sunsets (and sunrises too) and a 72-degree ocean with killer waves. We met surfers there from all over the world, although most were from the western United States. It was here that we spent Christmas, about as far away from the crowded freeways and malls of Southern California as we could get. It was also here that we adopted Gonzo—or he adopt-ed us. As he told you, he showed up on Christmas Eve, settled in for a nap in the shade under the motor home and we fell in love with him ... on the spot.

I wasn't ready to leave Todos Santos, but then I would have preferred an 18-week (or month) trip to an 18-day one. Who wouldn't? From there we drove back up north to Loreto, where we camped in town and enjoyed the beach, restaurants and shopping. Because Loreto has an international airport and has been targeted by Fonatur, Mexico's tourism agency, for development into a major resort, there are great restaurants and nightlife. Built in 1697, its mission, "*Nuestra Señora de Loreto. Cabeza y Madre de las Misiones de Baja y Alta California*—Our Lady of Loreto. Head and Mother of the Missions of Lower and Upper California"—is a historical landmark. It was the first mission as well as the first permanent settlement in either Baja or Alta California, and is considered the birthplace of the Californias.

Baja is rich in history from the Missionary Era, which began in the early 1500s and ended 300 years later when all the missions were secularized by the Mexican government. While Cortez, Ulloa, Vizcaíno and Cabrillo all explored the peninsula, it wasn't until Father Juan María Salvatierra, a Jesuit priest, landed in Loreto in 1697 that a permanent settlement was established in Baja. The Jesuits built a total of 18 missions from 1697 - 1767 when the Franciscans, under Father Junipero Serra, took over. He established only one mission in Baja before moving north to San Diego and Alta California.

The Franciscans ceded the Baja missions to the Dominicans in 1773 and in the next six decades, the Dominicans built nine more missions in Baja. By then, however, the population of native Indians had shrunk (due to death by warfare and disease) to only a fraction of its original number, so there was no longer an economically feasible reason for the existence of the missions. By 1846 the era of the missions was over. Some have disappeared. Most are in ruins; but a few—like Loreto, Mulegé, San José del Cabo, San Javier and San Ignacio have been restored—and house active parishes today.

When we were there, Derek and I got up early one morning to take Gonzo for a walk. The dog wasn't good on a leash yet, and he pretty much dragged us down to the malecón, where we found a bench facing the ocean and sat down to watch the rest of the sunrise. We let him loose to run on the beach. So quickly that it seemed like our eyes were betraying us, the sky turned from pale lavender laced with hot pink to a deep, wild shade of purple and vibrant fuchsia. The gold around the edges melted into a bright orange. Like a sunset in reverse, the sun popped up over the edge of the water and rose all at once—a huge red ball of fire in the sky. A lone pelican sailed by on a smoothly curving current of air about 12 feet above sea level. "You know what?" I said to Derek, "In my next life, I want to come back as a pelican." He rolled his eyes at me.

I was telling the truth. I adore pelicans. They're a curious, unlikely mixture of clumsiness and grace—like most humans. We sat together, watching as another pelican took off from the rocks in front of us, pushing the air with his feet. When he'd achieved altitude, he caught the current and started to glide with it. He joined up with seven more and they organized themselves into a V formation and swirled around to catch a higher current.

"I've always wondered if they can actually see the air," I told my son. "It all appears so effortless, but can you just imagine how much fun it would be? When they're hungry, they skim low over the waves, looking for food. When they see something that looks appetizing, they zoom up. They zoom down. They dive bomb. Watch!"

Two pelicans aimed themselves at the water and landed with splashes that exploded at least six feet into the air. "When they come up, if you look really carefully, you'll be able to tell if they got their fish," Derek informed me. He's always known more about wild creatures than anyone I know—having been a devotee of the Discovery Channel since he was a toddler.

"How?"

"There. Now. The one on the left. Watch his entire body shiver as he tosses his head back and flips that fish from his pouch into his mouth and sends it sliding on down his throat. But Mom, you can't come back as a pelican. You hate fish!"

After breakfast, we went to the mission. Right next to it is the *Museo de las Misiones*, a historical and anthropological museum. An impressionistic statue of Christ on the cross, carved from driftwood is in the centerpiece of the courtyard, near wine presses and an ox cart.

I dragged everyone into the museum. It was built with materials indigenous to the region: stone, brick, shell lime, mesquite, palm and ironwood. There are a few priceless old oil paintings that look like they belong in museum in Europe, rather than this remote Baja village over 700 miles south of the border. The museum's ethnographic collection offers samples of the region's arts and crafts. There's a boat hand-hewn from a single log, saddles, horse-hair halters and clothing typical of that worn by people in the missionary period. The kids were bored, but for me, I had a startling flash of what life must have been like for the missionaries on this peninsula 300 years ago.

Outside, a bust of Padre Salvatierra, founder of Loreto, faced us from a plaza across the street. What had once been the main street of town is now a pedestrian walkway. And yes, Gayle dragged me into each of the shops in the mall.

The next day we were off to Guerrero Negro, where we hooked up with Baja Jones Whale Adventure Tours and spent New Year's Eve morning, 1999 on Laguna Ojo de Liebre cruising in a panga alongside gray whales. For 45 minutes our boat followed a mama and newborn calf as we all watched the baby gradually gain strength and learn to swim on his own. At first he could barely hold his head above water and was forced to lay sideways across his mom's back while she held him up so he could breathe. By the time the pair pulled away from another approaching panga, the baby was able to swim freely alongside his mother. The rapture on my kids' faces as they sat in the front of the panga is something I will never, ever forget.

That night we were treated to the most astonishing fireworks celebration any of us had ever seen. It lasted for 75 minutes, there were two towers of pinwheels, two and three stories high and there were six mini-finales before the "grand finale." My kids sat on a wall, surrounded by Mexican children, snapping photos as fast as they could. Our group of 23 was the only group of gringos around for this celebration put on by the salt operation (jointly owned by the Mexican Government and Mitsubishi). Later, we went on to a fiesta at the Fundadora where we were also the only group of gringos. It didn't matter. When midnight struck, everyone in sight hugged me or shook my hand, wishing me a "Happy New Year" or a "Feliz Año." It didn't even matter that I was in jeans and they were in semi-formal to formal attire.

The next morning we got up and drove to La Bufadora. It took nearly nine hours, but we were able to spend the last day and a half of our trip visiting old friends and enjoying the amenities of my sister's Baja casita. Did we have fun? Absolutely. Would we do it again? Of course. My only complaint is one I've already voiced, and that is that we didn't have 18 weeks....

Terry and Antonio at the Mayan Kululkan temple at Chichén Itzá.

Sidetracked: Visiting Antonio and La Riviera Maya
February 2001

Back when Europe was locked deep in the dark ages, the Mayans were thriving, their culture both sophisticated and diverse. The five Maya nations were originally located in Belize, El Salvador, Guatemala, Honduras and Mexico, and although their cities were abandoned approximately 450 years ago and fell to ruin, they are still thriving as a people. Today they inhabit the Mexican states of Tabasco, Campeche, Chiapas, Yucatan and Quintana Roo.

I know this is a long way from Baja, but every once in a while you have to get sidetracked. Branch off. We did this. We finally got to take that romantic airplane vacation. We went to visit a friend from Baja who'd moved to Cancún.

If you make a trip to Cancún, or any of the other resorts nearby on the Yucatan peninsula, you'll be surrounded by the Maya. They still farm the land and live in small villages throughout the Yucatan peninsula—much as they did centuries ago. They own and work in the shops where you'll buy handicrafts or groceries, the restaurants where you'll eat and the hotels where you'll stay. They are a friendly and proud people. If you're interested, it's possible they'll teach you a few words in their language. For sure, you'll have to try some of their unique cuisine.

For the Maya, eating has always been an act of spirituality. Their foods are different than those served in northern Mexico, and most Americans and other tourists are unfamiliar with them. Their chile of choice is the habanero, the hottest chile known to mankind. It is revered for its healing powers and supposedly will ward off any number of illnesses. I swear that it gives off the best endorphin rush of any chile.

The first night of February 2001 we took the "Red Eye" from Los Angeles to Miami. From there we flew into Cancún. Antonio, who used to own the coolest Mexican handcraft shop in the La Bufadora Mall, picked us up at the airport. He delivered us to our hotel in Cancún, after which we did some beach time, caught a few winks and headed out to explore the city.

Next morning, Antonio picked us up early and we headed off to Chichén Itzá to visit the ruins of the incredible Mayan Kululkan temple. En route we stopped at the colonial town of Vallodolid to buy an authentic Yucatecan hand-embroidered blouse.

Every spring and fall, on the exact date of the solar equinox, people come from all over to the Kululkan Pyramid to witness watch what's known as the "Equinox Solar Phenomena." Without fail, on these days, the shadow of a snake ascends or descends the steps of the pyramid—precisely, on time and without fail. That is because the Mayans developed their own accurate calendar, and were able to exactly predict both equinoxes.

The three of us climbed the pyramid that day. The heat was intense. The stairs were steep, but narrow in width—obviously designed for people with a lot smaller feet than ours. When I reached the top, I was struck with a dizzying case of vertigo. How in the world would I get down those steep, narrow steps? I watched a few timid people like me. They were going down like crabs, sitting on one step and then lowering themselves down to the next one on all fours. Looked like it would work for me, so I went down on my butt too.

Other structures at Chichén Itzá include the Temple of the Warriors, the Temple of the Jaguars, El Mercado, Caracol, also known as the Observatory and the Ball Court (the largest in Mesoamerica).

Looking out over the area, you immediately know what an amazing civilization the Maya were.

After lunch at a roadside café, where I scarfed down the absolute best salsa (habanero) of my life, we went on to visit the Cenote Ik'kil. There is no adequate way to describe a cenote. You have to experience it to believe it. Beneath the Yucatan peninsula is a network of underground rivers and countless naturally occurring, crystal clear pools of the purest, most refreshing water imaginable. You can snorkel and dive in them. You can picnic next to them. They are not to be missed.

Cenote Ik'kil is privately owned. Of all the cenotes we visited, it was by far the most spectacular. The grounds were elegantly landscaped and meticulously maintained. Descending down a stone stairway to at least 200 feet below the surface, we reached the cenote. Its steep walls were covered in vines and roots. Sunlight poured in from an opening above, as did a waterfall and dangling greenery. There was a diving platform. There was a restroom and changing area, so we put on our swimsuits, dove in and swam for almost an hour. It was beyond awesome.

The next day, Antonio dropped us off at the ferry to Isla Mujeres, a tiny island about 25 minutes off the shore of Cancún. A quiet island village, Isla is not to be missed. It reminded me of Mexico from way back, when we were kids. The beaches are pristine and go on for what feels like forever. The shopping is great. The restaurants are great. The people are laid back and will chat with you for as long as you like. There are plenty of bars and restaurants right on the sand where you can relax in a hammock while listening to live music.

We took the ferry back to Cancún the next morning … way too soon for us. A visit to Isla Mujeres should last at least a week. Antonio picked us up at the dock and took us to Gran Cenote, where we snorkeled with neon tetra fish and swam among tropical greenery and underwater limestone formations. Through our dive masks we watched a pair of divers descend into underwater caves, and kept watching until their lights dimmed and then disappeared into the darkness.

From there it was onto Tulúm, another Mayan city right on the Caribbean. A walled city, it was home to the Mayan priests and other elite up until about 400 years ago. It's another magical place….

Then, we visited the X'Cacel (pronounced EESH-kah-sell)

reef. Antonio and I snorkeled along the coral reef, swimming with an array of tropical fish and even a sea turtle.

Our next stop was our longest. After four days of dashing about, visiting incredible places, we were ready for some serious rest, relaxation and beach time. We'd booked four nights in a little palapa on the edge of the Caribbean at a place called the Blue Parrot Inn in Playa del Carmen. Playa, as everyone down there calls it, is the hot spot on the Riviera Maya these days. A mere 40 minute ride from the Cancún airport, it's easily accessible, but not crowded or crazy. It's one of the most welcoming, friendly places either of us has ever been. We loved it—every single moment of it. We checked into our room, unpacked and headed off down the beach, flip-flops in hand. We followed the music to a beachside bar where a reggae band was playing. The sun had just set and the light was fading from the still-opalescent sky. I said, "I think we've just arrived in adult summer camp!"

For four days, we got up, put on our bathing suits (and for me, a *pareo*—sarong), and headed out to find a new restaurant for breakfast. Our only rule in Playa was that we wouldn't eat at the same restaurant twice. There were way too many to choose from to duplicate. All the restaurants were indoor/outdoor. All were gorgeous. All served delicious food … and at night … many of them had live (no cover charge anytime) music!

We ate authentic Mayan food. We ate scrumptious seafood (well, Terry did), elegant flambéed steak and casual but delicious street tacos (of course). Every meal we ate was at least as good as the meal before—and it wasn't expensive.

And the music! Ah, the music! How great is the music in Playa? Well, Playa is very small. Its main street, Avenida Quinta (or Fifth Avenue) becomes, at night, a veritable "street scene." People on foot cruise up and down the street. The sounds of live music pour from at least every other restaurant. People are dining al fresco or shopping in one of the many colorful shops selling Mexican arts, crafts and clothing.

We cruised, we dined, and we searched for music. We always found it. We heard a great blues band with a lady sax player. We danced to authentic Cuban music, played by real Cubans. We heard reggae bands, rock'n roll, calypso, plenty of Mariachi music and the haunting tunes of the Andes.

One day we rented bikes and toured the area, from Coco

Beach to the north to Playa Car with its upscale golf course and fancy five-star hotels to the south. We made friends. We swam. We lazed. We enjoyed. Our four days were up way, way too soon. So we will be back, for sure. We want to spend a month or two, visit every cenote we can and seep ourselves in the culture and ambience of the Riviera Maya. And everywhere else in Mexico I haven't been yet....

* * * *

Postscript:
        Because this is one of my favorite recipes, and I created it after this trip, Mayan Salsa Habanera is not in my cookbook. It's hot, but not overwhelmingly so. Don't be a wimp. Habanero chiles are good for you. To make a quick and easy nacho dish that will tantalize your taste buds, spread a bunch of tortilla chips on a plate. Top with grated cheese. Microwave for about a minute, then top with this salsa. Hint: Preparation time for the salsa is about 30 minutes and the recipe makes about a pint.

Mayan Salsa Habanera
1 large red onion, finely diced
6 large tomatoes, finely diced
1 bunch cilantro, chopped
3 cloves garlic, minced
4 habanero chiles, minced
juice of 2 limes
1 tbsp orange juice
1 tbsp Controy (Cointreau or Triple Sec can be substituted)
1 tbsp salt

Mix all ingredients together in bowl. Cover and refrigerate for up to three days. Use with chips, on tacos or as a condiment to any Mexican dish.

Part Four: Tips For Traveling in Baja

Tecolote Beach near La Paz
Photo courtesy of Kit Worthington

The Basics...

I wrote my second book, *Cartwheels in the Sand—Baja California, Four Women and a Motor Home* largely to explode the myth that women can't travel safely in Mexico. I haven't made the trip to Cabo with only women, but I drove a motor home to San Felipe with Susanne, another single mom and our three kids a few Spring Breaks ago. I drive all over Baja. I love making the trip to La Bufadora alone ... just me and my dogs ... singing at the top of my lungs and not bothering anyone!

First and foremost, follow my dad's advice and remember this always: You are a guest in a foreign country. Be courteous. Be respectful. Don't behave like a jerk. Obey the laws. But don't be afraid. I feel safer in Mexico than most places in the U.S. Treat the people with respect and they will overwhelm you with that famous "Baja Hospitality." If you're anxious about foreign travel or have heard negative stuff in the press, try picking up some Baja books. There's a lot to learn from other Americans who've spent time in Mexico, understand the people, the place, the culture and love it. Do a subject search on Baja or Mexico on Amazon.com.

Identification and Other Legal Entry Requirements...

U.S. citizens are not required to obtain a Visa to visit Mexico for up to 180 days. If traveling only as far as Ensenada or San Felipe in Baja, you will need a photo ID, such as a driver's license. If you are a citizen of another country, you will need to bring your passport and show legal permanent residency papers at port of entry.

If you are planning to go south of Ensenada or San Felipe, you will need to purchase a Tourist Card, which costs approximately $22 and is good for six months. In addition to a Tourist Card, if you are traveling south by car, RV, bus, cruise ship, or airplane, U.S. citizens are required to have a photo ID and a certified copy of your birth certificate or a passport. If you're flying or on a ship or other tour, the cost of the Tourist Card will be included in the price of your ticket. The airline or tour agency will provide the form and help you fill it out.

If you're on your own, you are responsible for getting your own Tourist Card. Any consulate of Mexico, the Mexican tourism offices, some travel agencies and Discover Baja Travel Club in San Diego can issue this card. You can reach Discover Baja at 1-800-727-BAJA.

If you don't have time to pick one up before you cross the border, you can stop in just south of the border in Tijuana to get a Tourist Card. In Ensenada, pick up a Tourist Card at the *Migración*—Immigration Office at the port. It's right on your way into town on the left-hand side of the road, across from the shipyard. Afterward, you will have to go to a local bank and pay your 195 peso fee.

Minors going to Mexico alone or accompanied by just one parent are required to present a notarized affidavit of permission from both parents or the absent parent at their point of entry.

As of September 14, 2001, citizens of certain specified Middle Eastern countries must apply for permission to enter Mexico at least six to eight weeks ahead of time. These people should contact the Mexican Consulate nearest them for more information.

Mexican Car Insurance...

Buy inexpensive Mexican car insurance at one of the drive-through agencies in San Ysidro just before you cross the border. All you need is a copy of your current vehicle registration and a valid driver's license. Some U.S. car rental companies allow you to drive their cars into Mexico, provided you purchase insurance beforehand. If you're planning to spend more than 10 days in Mexico, it's cheaper to buy a year's policy. An online search will yield many companies that provide insurance. Also ... make sure your policy includes legal coverage, in the event of an accident. Please, don't cross the border without Mexican car insurance!

Fishing Licenses, etc...

If you're planning to fish, on your own and not through a hotel or charter outfit, contact Discover Baja Travel Club for information at:
1-800-727-BAJA or DiscoverBaja.com

Money Matters...

The currency is the peso, which currently exchanges at the rate of approximately 9 x 1 to the U.S. dollar. However, dollars are accepted everywhere and there are ATMs (Cajas Permanente in Spanish) in front of many banks and in most large grocery stores. You can easily withdraw money from your U.S. account, but the money will be delivered to you in pesos.

What about drinking the Water?

General rule of thumb is ... don't drink tap water, unless you're in Todos Santos or the East Cape where the water is pure, pure, pure. Bottled water is used throughout Mexico for drinking water. It's safe.

And Getting Sick?

Another of my dad's favorite sayings is that Montezuma's Revenge is generally caused by: too much sun, too much booze and too much spicy food. The bottom line here is ... moderation. Try to avoid overdoing it. Unless you're a seasoned traveler, you may fall prey to First Night in Camp syndrome and find yourself benched for days. If that happens, send someone to a *farmacía*—pharmacy. There are medicines to help cut down the recovery time. Use sunscreen. Drink lots of water. Go easy on the chiles!

Where to Find More Information on Baja

By Phone:

Call Discover Baja Travel Club at 1-800-727-BAJA

On The Web:

The following list of websites is offered in alphabetical order. Although the list is not all-inclusive, several sites have search engine capabilities. All sites offer links to other related Baja sites.

Adobe Guadalupe—www.adobeguadalupe.com
Alfreda Communications—home.earthlink.net/~alfredacomm
Ann Hazard's Baja Magic—BajaMagic.com
Bahía de los Angeles—www.bajaexpo.com/cities/bahia
Baja Animal Sanctuary (Rosarito)—bajadogs.org
Baja California Language College—bajacal.com
Baja California Travel Resource Guide—escapist.com/baja
Baja Destinations—BajaDestinations.com
Baja Discovery Whale Tours—bajadiscovery.com
Baja Expeditions—www.bajaex.com

Baja Jones Whale and Cave Painting tours—www.greywhale.com
Baja Life Magazine—www.bajalife.com
Bajalinks: Books, Newspapers, Publications—bajalinks.com
Baja Nomad—www.bajanomad.com
Baja Portal—bajaportal.com
Baja Quest—www.bajaquest.com/index.html
Baja Traveler Magazine—bajamagazine.com
Baja Web—bajaweb.com
Cabo San Lucas—allaboutcabo.com
Cabo San Lucas—cabosanlucas.com
Carlos Fiesta's Baja Expo—BajaExpo.com
Discover Baja CaliforniaTravel Club—discoverbaja.com
Ecomundo (Bahía Concepción)—home.earthlink.net/~rcmathews
Ensenada—ensenada.net.mx/gazette
Ensenada Wine Growers' Association—Ensenadawines.com
Foxploratioan—www.foxploration.com
Fox Studios Baja—www.foxbaja.com
Galería Santini (Rosarito)—giorgiosantini.com
Guerrero Negro—baja.com/negro
Hotel Buena Vista Beach Resort (the Spa)—www.hotelbuenavista.com
La Bufadora—labufadora.com
La Paz—www.bajaquest.com/lapaz
Loreto—www.loreto.com
Los Cabos—loscabos.com
MEXICO OnLine—www.mexonline.com
Mulegé—www.mulege.com
Pancho's Restaurant and Tequila Bar—www.panchos.com
People's Guide to Mexico—www.peoplesguide.com
Rosarito Beach—rosaritobch.com
San Diego Natural History Museum—www.sdnhm.org
San Felipe—www.sanfelipe.com.mx
San Ignacio—www.bajalife.com/sanignacio
San Quintín—www.sanquintin.com
Tecate—www.bajalife.com/tecate
Tijuana—tijuana-net.com
Todos Santos-todossantos—baja.com or todossantos.cc

Travel Index

Renegade Enterprises Order Form

Agave Sunsets by Ann Hazard $19.95
Cartwheels in the Sand by Ann Hazard $14.95
Cooking with Baja Magic by Ann Hazard $21.95

Four easy ways to order:
1. Phone orders: 760-944-6711 (PST)
2. Fax orders: 760-944-6765
3. E-mail: Cookbaja@aol.com
4. Mail: Renegade Enterprises
         P.O. Box 1505
         Solana Beach, CA 92075

	Quantity Each	Total Books
Agave Sunsets	_____	_____
Cartwheels in the Sand	_____	_____
Cooking with Baja Magic	_____	_____
Subtotal	_____	_____
Shipping & Handling $3.95 per book (US)		_____
Add Sales Tax for delivery to CA: 7.75%		_____
TOTAL AMOUNT		_____

Enclosed is a check, money order or credit card information in the amount of:

$_____ payable to RENEGADE ENTERPRISES

___ Check or Money Order ___ Master Card ___ Visa

Account #_____ Expiration Date _____

Signature_____

Send book(s) to:
Name_____
Street Address_____
City/State/Zip_____
Daytime phone_____
E-mail_____